Divine Energy

Insight, Healing & Potential

Hazel Devine

with Susan Keenan

Copyright © 2022 Hazel Devine
All Rights Reserved.
ISBN 978-1-914225-78-9

All intellectual property rights, including copyright, design right and publishing rights, rest with the author. No part of this publication may be copied, reproduced, stored, or transmitted in any way, including any written, electronic, recording or photocopying without written permission of the author. The information in this book was correct at the time of publication. The author does not assume liability for loss or damage caused by errors or omissions.

Edited by Geraldine Walsh
Written with Susan Keenan
Cover design by Hazel's sister Vanessa Mooney
Published by Orla Kelly Publishing

Disclaimer

The publisher and the author are providing this book and its contents on an "as is" basis and make no representations or warranties of any kind with respect to this book or its contents. The publisher and the author disclaim all such representations and warranties, including but not limited to warranties of healthcare for a particular purpose. In addition, the publisher and the author assume no responsibility for errors, inaccuracies, omissions, or any other inconsistencies herein.

The content of this book is for informational purposes only and is not intended to diagnose, treat, cure, or prevent any condition or disease. You understand that this book is not intended as a substitute for consultation with a licensed practitioner. Please consult with your own physician or healthcare specialist regarding the suggestions and recommendations made in this book. The use of this book implies your acceptance of this disclaimer.

The publisher and the author make no guarantees concerning the level of success you may experience by following the advice and *strategies* contained in this book, and you accept the risk that results will differ for each individual. The testimonials and examples provided in this book show exceptional results, which may not apply to all readers, and are not intended to represent or guarantee that you will achieve the same or similar results.

About the Author

Hazel Devine is the second eldest of thirteen children. With five brothers and seven sisters, growing up in the Midlands in Ireland during the 60's and 70's was not particularly easy. As a highly sensitive child, Hazel was prone to sickness and illness in her early years and suffered convulsions and constant ear infections. Hazel recognises her mother's strength in raising her children during a time of financial and emotional stress. During her childhood, Hazel became aware of a keen alertness to other people's emotions, anxieties, and wellbeing. She struggled to understand or control this high level of sensitivity in her youth, leading her to suppress this natural intuitive gift. In her early 30's Hazel began to connect with her own life on a physical, mental, and emotional level as panic attacks and migraines took over due to significantly stressful life events. She practised energy healing, learned to develop, and focus her abilities and ultimately found her calling in life.

Hazel is a recognised Holistic Therapist focusing on energy awareness. As a mentor, she hosts workshops in self-development, self-awareness, healing, meditation, and more. As a guide and a teacher, she helps others navigate their lives to find their own voice. Her special ability to read peoples physical, emotional, and mental health based on their energy is evident from the wide support she receives from clients who are eternally grateful to have crossed her path. Her patrons showcase their admiration for her work in guiding them to gain confidence in their self-belief and abilities.

By connecting the moments in our lives, processing our emotions, and allowing the power of healing energy into our lives, Hazel encourages us to look honestly at what prevents us from moving forward, finding the blocks, and becoming agents of change in our own lives.
Divine Energy: Insight, Healing & Potential is Hazel's first book.

Website: HazelDevine.com
Facebook @HazelDevineEnergyAwareness
Instagram @HazelDevineEnergy
Linkedin:Hazel Devine
Email: hazeldevine@gmail.com

Testimonials

Ann says, "The minute I sat down with Hazel, she was able to tell me exactly what was happening to me."
I heard of Hazel Devine from a friend who thought she would do me good. I had experienced sibling rivalry for a few years while caring for my elderly mother. This affected my blood pressure and self-confidence. I was questioning myself and feeling insecure. The minute I sat down with Hazel, she was able to tell me exactly what was happening to me and how I was being isolated by my family. She advised me on how to bring up my energy and stand up for myself to say what I wanted. Hazel told me that I am a very caring person, which I always have tried to be. This gave me back my confidence and belief in myself. I have had many sessions with Hazel over the years, and after each session, I have come home relieved of all stress and aches and feeling able to handle family situations. I would highly recommend Hazel.

Carol says, "Hazel has always been honest, accepting and understanding, always delivering truth and in a way that I could hear and understand."
I've known Hazel now for over ten years. I remember my first session and how seen and understood I felt. Hazel saw and read my energy and helped me to understand myself and my sensitivity. That day left a lasting impression on me and was the beginning of my own learning journey of healing and personal growth.

Hazel has helped, guided, and supported me through making changes in my life, facing fears as they came up, giving guidance and direction as needed. Hazel has always been honest, accepting and understanding, always delivering truth and in a way that I could hear and understand. She has given me the clarity to understand emotional and physical pain, and this has helped physical symptoms to clear and allowed me to break old habits and patterns in my life.

Hazel's energy work and abilities to heal have helped me gain an understanding of myself and others. Through practising the energy skills I've learned over the years, I've come to know who I am and have gained confidence and self-belief in my own abilities.

More recently, I've attended Hazel's meditation classes online and in person. I've noticed a calmness and peace of mind from taking part in these classes. She has helped me through some of the most difficult times of my life. I am incredibly grateful to her.

Josephine says, "Hazel's energy is like that of an ideal maternal love, welcoming, wholesome, comforting, and compassionate. She epitomises the word love."

I met Hazel over 12 years ago. I was extremely impressed by her gift of insight, healing power and above all, her ability to deliver a message with kindness and love. Over the years, I have seen Hazel in a private capacity as well as working closely with her in a group setting. She has the ability to say something in a simple way, and when I consider it honestly, it is the key to clarity, healing, and successful decision-making in any given circumstance. Sometimes I struggle with what I hear, but she is always honest, and I appreciate that level of integrity.

I have come a long way and enjoy a balanced life now on many levels. Hazel has helped me work through my emotional wounds to become the person I am today, and I am still growing.

I would recommend Hazel if you have any emotional, physical, or mental health issues or concerns. If you want to help yourself, step out of your comfort zone and visit Hazel. She will give you her time, healing, and energy, allowing you to change your life. Hazel's energy is like that of an ideal maternal love, welcoming, wholesome, comforting, and compassionate. She epitomises the word love.

Mary says, "Hazel is very intuitive, insightful, and she has a very special gift."
I initially heard about Hazel through my chiropodist, and I texted for an appointment. At the time, there was a waiting list, so I attended one of her workshops. I remember Hazel got delayed, but when she arrived, she was straight into the delivery. She knew nothing about me. Firstly she got us to pick a card, and from the card we picked, she was able to tell us about our lives. I and the other members of the group were absolutely amazed by her accuracy.

Hazel is very intuitive, insightful and she has an incredibly special gift. I have had phone sessions with Hazel which I love as she always gives me especially useful feedback and a healing to complete my session. I recommended her to my daughter, who has taken her son for a healing with amazing results. I would highly recommend Hazel.

Paula says, "Through her workshops and meditations, Hazel created a safe space for me to grow and be really true to myself."
Since starting my journey with Hazel years ago, stepping onto the hard road of really looking within myself through her self-development course, my life has changed forever. Hazel has supported me on this path, unlocking and nurturing my natural abilities. Through her workshops and meditations, Hazel created a safe space for me to grow and be really true to myself. Her divine abilities and knowledge come from pure light, and her guidance helped me advance to the level where I am starting my own practice. I am forever grateful to my teacher Hazel.

Noeleen says, "Hazel truly helped me with her effective, humble, realistic, and honest approach."

Hazel Divine has supported me since 2008 and guided me to empower myself and to practice a healthier belief system. Hazel truly helped me with her effective, humble, realistic, and honest approach. I have a medical and holistic background. Medication can numb the pain; counselling can bring up the pain. She showed me how to look at my thoughts and beliefs and how my emotions were affecting my body. She allowed me to see how my self-destructive thoughts were bringing up physical pain. Hazel helped me to change my negative thinking and cut old behaviour patterns and habits, allowing me to connect with the real source of myself.

Hazel has supported me in many ways, such as with issues of fertility. I was told a year prior to a fertility appointment that I would have to have a hysterectomy, following tests for my ongoing gynaecological problems. This was a massive shock as I was in my early twenties at the time. I was told on a Thursday by my doctor that I couldn't have children. The following Monday, my first appointment was with Hazel. She empowered my belief system that day to be open to another mindset. Over a number of sessions, this unblocked negative energy stored in my womb and ovaries. Mind over matter! No truer a saying from my experience. I now have a beautiful girl. Obstetricians were shocked.

A few major events occurred together involving loss. I experienced the death of a parent and a toxic relationship in my marriage, and I lost my sense of myself again. Hazel empowered me to accept and maintain a gentle approach to finding my identity and purpose. I became a survivor instead of continuing to practice old coping mechanisms, which were evidently toxic, making me a victim and keeping me stuck in a negative cycle.

I now attract more positive people and experiences in my life. I am more aware of traumatic negative cycles in my family circle stemming from childhood. I look at these and allow them to open and heal. This invaluable awareness and approach, along with practising healthy boundaries, has allowed me to decide that the negativity stops with me and does not influence my child's future decisions and experiences.

Realistically, Rome was not built in a day. Medical and holistic professionals have supported me in each healing phase. It's important to ask for support. You're not alone. Hazel's unique gift and healing approach has been a major healing platform for me. My time with her has encouraged me to accept that it is ok to be different and to stop people-pleasing. I have learned to reduce fears, identify panic moments and to stop looking for others approval. I'm not allowing myself to be manipulated or to manipulate others. I'm now allowing a healthier generation to evolve from the one in which I grew up. I can still have difficult days but knowing Hazel's awareness techniques has allowed me to step into the moment.

I'm so grateful I met Hazel, that I was open to asking for help, and that I continue to when I need it. I feel that the more I practice her healing techniques and affirmations, I will only move forward and not backwards ever again.

This book is dedicated to my parents Phylis and Paudge Mooney, my 12 siblings, Martina, Paddy, Mary, Margaret, Pamela, Veronica, Kevin, Derek, Anne, Alan, Vanessa and Joseph my sons, Vincent, Christopher, and Keith, and my beautiful grandchildren.

Contents

About the Author v
Testimonials vii
Foreword xix
Introduction 1
How to Use this Book 5

Part One: Understanding Who You Are 11

Chapter One: The Four Key Elements 13
Chapter Two: Life-Force Energy 23
Chapter Three: Sensitivity, Intuition & Listening 29
Chapter Four: The Power of Thinking 39
Chapter Five: Clearing the Impact of Others 49
Chapter Six: The Releasing Breath 57
Chapter Seven: Balancing the Body 64

Part Two: Looking at Yourself Honestly 71

Chapter One: The Value of Feelings and Learning to
 Manage our Feelings 73
Chapter Two: Sleep 89
Chapter Three: Arising Panic 96
Chapter Four: Connection and Disconnection 106
Chapter Five: Negativity 121

Chapter Six: Pain..135
Chapter Seven: Our Relationship with Food 142
Chapter Eight: Responsibility and Forgiving Others 148
Chapter Nine: Trauma...157
Chapter Ten: Personalities..183
Chapter Eleven: Depression..197

Part Three: Building Foundations for a Wonderful Life 209
Chapter One: How to Value Yourself....................................211
Chapter Two: Friendships and Relationships........................225
Chapter Three: Learning 234
Chapter Four: Your Time 242
Chapter Five: The Amazing Gift of Life................................247

Part Four: Healing Practices 261
Practice One: Grounding 263
Practice Two: Five Finger Breathing 267
Practice Three: The Calm Breath 269
Practice Four: The Rope of Life...271
Practice Five: The Bubble Meditation 276
Practice Six: Healing Meditation for our Bones....................278
Practice Seven: Loving Heart Meditation 283
Practice Eight: Healing Lungs Meditation 289
Practice Nine: Deep Meditation..293
    A Final Note..297
    Resources 300
    Acknowledgements..304
    Please Review 307

A special acknowledgement to Susan Keenan for her excellent writing skills, her input, dedication and time given to writing this book.

Foreword

As the second oldest of six children, with cousins living next door and my mother caring for and fostering children, our family always felt bigger than it was. With so much responsibility, my parents instilled strong values in us all, including helping others and working hard, as we grew up in a busy home.

I was an extremely sensitive child, constantly aware of how others around me were feeling. I had particular difficulty being immersed in the volume of emotions in school. To balance the intensity, I instinctively spent as much time as I could outside helping out on my uncle's farm. But I was often anxious, sensing other people's stress, impatience, and sadness. So much so, I often carried it as my own. I feared not being able to deal with issues in the moment and of being judged by others. Though often overwhelmed by situations, I became an expert at hiding my insecurities.

When it came to school and college, I studied extra hard, overcompensating for those uncertainties. As I trained to be a teacher and began my career, I over-prepared lessons to avoid being overcome and anxious. Soon after, with my husband, Kevin, we travelled a little and moved to Cork for ten years. There I studied yoga and energy healing which gave me a glimpse into the healing power of energy. Then, with our two beautiful daughters, we decided to move back to the midlands so we could be closer to family as the girls grew up.

After the birth of our third child, I came home from hospital with my new baby, ready to enjoy this new life, getting to know him and watching his sisters' excitement at having a little brother. However, things were not to be so straightforward. All the anxiety I had held in my body up to that point in my life had suddenly opened. It was a flood of anxiety. As I focused on the anxiousness, memories surged. I felt each one deeply as if I were there again, as if all past troubling memories were suddenly present all at once. I couldn't sleep for the next two weeks. Most nights, I wouldn't sleep at all; others, I would catch one or two hours. I had terrifying nightmares. I was exhausted, but every time I lay down, I felt as though I was losing control of my mind. After a GP appointment, I was on mild medication, which helped me sleep each night, but Hazel helped me climb up out of this flood of emotion.

When I tried to explain or talk about how scared I felt, the words wouldn't come. My thoughts were blocked, but as Hazel tuned into me, she accurately described how I felt. She could see the rush of anxiety flooding my body, the physical pain I was experiencing, and my fears for the future. She laid it all out for me - my feelings, thoughts, and pain. Hazel understood, but more so, she could feel what it was like to be me, in my body, going through all of this. She looked at me and, with great conviction and presence, told me I was going to be okay, and I believed her. I will always be grateful to her for this moment. The relief was immense. It took me another three or four months to recover, and I still had difficult days, but I had found my courage and a belief in my own strength.

Regularly attending Hazel's workshops and continuing my learning with her about using energy to benefit myself and others has been life-changing. I learned how to be present and separate all I feel, trust my knowledge, and let go of the feelings that are not mine. I started working through my past experiences allowing suppressed emotions, thoughts, and physical pain to come up and be released. I am still acutely aware of how people around me are feeling. My system can sometimes be flooded by people with strong personalities who carry a lot of pain or by a volume of smaller interactions when

I allow myself to get tired. However, I now see the value of my sensitivity which allows me to look at situations with clarity. I can give back others' emotions, stand in my strength, deal with my own feelings and thoughts, and quickly recover. I practice breath work and create space around me which lessens other people's emotional impact on me. I enjoy meditation and the replenishment it gives me when I let go of thought and feel the stillness and power of presence and my connection to creativity and inspiration.

Life is exciting. I am continuously amazed by the power of energy healing and the freedom and strength people experience when they let go of past experiences stored in the body. May you feel acknowledged as you read Divine Energy: Insight, Healing & Potential. May you bring practices into your life that allow you to relax into being yourself and feel the presence of your power.

Susan Keenan

Introduction

Hello, and you are very welcome! It's exciting to be sharing with you the information and energy that has come to me through my healing work on myself and others over the last eighteen years.

We live in a time bridging from an older, more rigid way of looking at things where roles and heavy expectations were placed on people to a kinder, more authentic way of being. Government, religion, and traditional views had put an inflexible structure on how we lived, but this is changing and bringing with it some upheaval. Things that were hidden, such as abuse, corruption, and neglect, are coming out into the light. This can make our world feel a little chaotic as people build a new structure in their lives.

Concurrently as older world views are being left behind, we are inundated with information and new expectations. We are bombarded with social media and phones that constantly seek our attention. We have been swept up into a faster pace of life. Pressure in our work, education, relationships, and family life has increased. We are juggling many responsibilities and activities. People's image online is often valued over truth, real kindness, and wisdom. Expectations are put upon us to succeed in our lives, but the set of conditions that define what family or society deem as success may not actually be what brings us happiness or fulfilment. Our sense of community has been weakened as we live more individual lives. Financial pressures abound.

Interwoven through this, we all have our own internal world to deal with. Traditionally our internal struggles were hidden or downplayed. We have struggles such as anxiety, panic, loneliness, disconnection, obsessive thoughts, negative thinking, depression, guilt, trauma, shock, physical pain, illness, fertility problems, addictions, eating disorders, grief, stress, relationship difficulties, dishonesty, unconscious habits, self-doubt, or a lack of purpose.

We can find ourselves, to varying extents, following what we think others expect or what we have decided to expect of ourselves, living as a false image of ourselves, too busy or fearful to stand back and take a look at who we really are or at the anxiety and confusion that we carry with us. How would our internal world be if we released our pain and remembered our value and worth, our true needs and desires and the qualities and potential within us to live a self-defined, great life? How would our collective external world be if a tipping point of individuals started to live from that place?

I have a particularly clear view of the baggage you could let go of and how you could embrace your potential.

I was born with a gift. I can feel, see, and hear in heightened ways. This allows me to give people clarity about the origin of problems with their physical, emotional, and mental health. I can provide them with insight into current situations in their lives and a new understanding around the impact of past experiences, experiences they couldn't process at the time that remained stuck in the initial impact of the event, in their bodies.

It took time for me to learn how to live in the world, feeling, seeing, and hearing things that no one around me could. Being so sensitive and different, you can imagine that my childhood wasn't the easiest. I was full of anxiety, always upset for everyone around me and very shy. In school, I just didn't fit in. I was constantly overwhelmed by the emotions and thoughts of my classmates and suffered from earaches and stomach upset. I had frequent headaches due to my father's depression and my mother's anxiety. Information that I just knew intuitively about other people, around their health or worries, was generally not welcome, and I was encouraged by the adults in my family to keep it to myself. Being the second oldest of thirteen, I took on a weight of responsibility as a minder in my family. I left school early and worked hard in factory jobs and allowed my gift to dim so I could lessen the impact of others around me.

I got married in my twenties. My marriage was tense as we both had our issues. The dynamic between us and the responsibility of being a young parent triggered memories from my past that I was unable to cope with. As a result, I suffered from depression and ill health, and was hospitalised several times for panic attacks, anaemia, and severe migraines. In my late thirties, my marriage ended. Counselling helped me through these years. I started to look at my experiences with a new awareness, learning not to stay stuck in them but to take the learning and insights they offered. I gradually saw that I could stop living in old family patterns and in the energy of my anxieties. My gift started opening up again, and I was ready to embrace it and trust what I could see, hear, and feel this time. I used it to look within myself to where anxieties, negativity, and depression started; to breathe into the places in my body where I had stored old emotions, especially my heart, stomach, and lower back and release these trapped feelings; to connect to the thinking patterns and habits that were no longer serving me well, causing panic and migraines, and change my thoughts and beliefs. Most significantly, I experienced the power of energy healing and how I could direct its flow to bring my body, emotions, and mind into balance and a state of well-being. I learned to relax the muscles of my body and allow my circulation to flow with ease. I learned to trust in myself, and once that was my way of being, nothing could hold me back. I began to shed others' judgements about what I could do and instead believe in myself and remember who I really am.

I am a listener, a spiritual but very practical teacher, an energy healer and also a medium. I took ownership of these aspects of myself and was ready to use my gift to empower others. I intuitively sense how people feel physically in their bodies and their emotional state, seeing images of their physical health by the way their energy flows through them. I hear spirit speak to me, telling me what people need to know and understand, and I can read a person's thinking patterns. I share my insights with kindness, compassion, and empathy. I don't judge people. I have guides around me. Some are constant, and others change alongside my teaching and learning. They step forward into my awareness as I need them. A number of them have helped with this project.

I'm also aware of the loving energy of angels. Their presence feels like a soft breeze that brings strength and courage. If you haven't any personal experience with the spirit world, don't worry; this is a book of practical guidance, so none is necessary to gain from this read.

How to Use this Book

Divine Energy: Insight, Healing & Potential is divided into four parts. I recommend reading the entire book to benefit from the flow of ideas and energy through it. Then you'll be familiar with its layout and can reread the sections which resonate most with your life experience and develop a regular practice of the breath work and meditations, which you will find beneficial.

Throughout the book, you will find *Journal Exercises* to help you explore how each topic relates to you. Answering these questions will give you clarity about where you are in relation to that topic and what you could resolve, release, or give to yourself to bring in more well-being, strength, peace, love, light, and healing into your life.

A section called *Stepping Back* is included within chapters that share with you times in my life when I experienced a particular topic or concept.

You will also find *Key Things to Remember* at the end of every chapter, which helps focus our thoughts on the important insights of each topic.

Part One - Understanding Who You Are

Part one of this book is a mini-course of what I have learned and used to balance my own life and help bring the lives of my clients into balance. It is an introduction to seeing ourselves more clearly and learning to stand as ourselves with both strength and ease. We will explore what it would be like for you if you took full ownership of your life, trusted, and acted on your intuition, really believed in your worth and felt a connection to inspiration. I will introduce you to the concept and power of life-force energy and how you can practice bringing up your energy daily to raise your sense of well-being.

We will look at your level of sensitivity and how you can use the calm breath to prevent being overwhelmed by others and instead use the gift of insight that your sensitivity brings. As an introduction to presence, we'll take a look at the concept of listening, and you can become aware of how you listen and also how you can communicate so that others can really understand what you need to say.

Next, we'll delve into thinking, the flow of words and images that are constantly moving and flashing through our minds. The various ways we process thoughts are very interesting, and I hope to convince you of the value of mind maintenance and of taking a few minutes to process your thoughts on a daily basis. Then we'll look at one of the most effective tools of well-being, clearing the impact of others. Learning to clear others' strong feelings and thoughts will have such a positive impact on you. I find that when we let go of what we have taken on from others, we can deal with our own lives. To help you do just that, we'll explore the power of breath work to help you release what you need to both enjoy and function well in your daily life.

Next, in this section, we will learn how to feel balanced and centred in ourselves. We'll finish with some power as we create a foundational platform underneath ourselves made up of our support network, our cherished values, constructive beliefs, and sources of strength. It gives us an effective structure so that we can cope well with whatever presents in our lives.

Part Two - Looking at Yourself Honestly

In part two, I invite you to go deeper. I want to take you by the hand and dive bravely with you into yourself so that you can take a clear and honest look at the things you struggle with. The recurring thoughts and stuck emotions tied to various experiences that are sapping your energy, affecting your thinking and physical health, and holding you back. So often, our reaction may be to suppress difficult thoughts and feelings, hide them away and try to pretend that we are fine, convincing ourselves something did not happen or that it's not affecting us. However, we are not built to cope with long-term avoidance.

Our bodies and minds are not able to hold huge amounts of emotions and accumulations of thought and function healthily and happily. It's time to look at, understand, and release the old patterns you have been carrying around. You may be surprised to realise some of these difficulties never belonged to you but carried over from other people around you at the time. I will support you to sit with any pain and have the courage to travel to where it started, to feel that moment and acknowledge it.

As a constriction of stuck emotions and thoughts is unknotted and released, pure love and powerful presence are given the opportunity to flow into that space. Then you will find that memories can set themselves back into their proper place in the past, and you are free of the suffering they were causing. Ease, wellness, joy, and a sense of being able to cope comes to the fore.

We'll do this one topic at a time at your pace, starting with the energy of feelings and how they flow or get stuck in our bodies. If you are a worrier, you'll relate to how worry intensifies in the body and how to resolve worrying. We'll look in particular at negative obsessive thoughts, their cause, and the key to releasing them. We all have regrets held in the body, and I'll share with you what I've learned about dealing with guilt in a step-by-step way.

We'll practise transitioning from our day to a restful night's sleep, and I'll give you clarity around nightmares. We'll explore how panic rises in our bodies and getting through the distress of panic attacks. We'll pause between topics for breath work and meditations to bring ourselves into balance. We'll view the concept of connection and discover the impact and causes of loneliness, negativity, stagnancy, hormone shifts, and pain in our lives. We'll delve into how we manage responsibility and into our ability to forgive others. We'll look at our relationship with food. Then we will traverse a level deeper and gain insights that will help us as we find our way through the most intense and heavy energy we carry - shock, trauma, addiction, grief, the impact of being bullied, taking on false personalities and losing our real selves, depression, and suicidal thoughts.

Throughout this section, I describe snippets of my life so you can see that I have personal experience with these states and therefore have true empathy with you. Along with the guidance and insights here, you will benefit from real-life support to address and release what you carry, so reach out to whomever you need, friends and family, support groups. See the resources section for some suggestions or visit your doctor or counsellor. There is no extra credit for resolving your struggles on your own.

Part Three - Building Foundations for a Wonderful Life

Building Foundations for a Wonderful Life is all about taking ownership of ourselves. It's about finding and constructing our steady place, a structured platform, a strong backbone within us, starting from an honest place. The key to this is making the decision to value ourselves. We will look at how others act as a mirror to us, highlighting our qualities and weaknesses and learning to use this constructively to decide what to build on and what to release. Let's shine a light on the harsh criticism that we subject ourselves to when we compare ourselves critically with others, and by looking at our reasons for this, let this habit go.

We will explore our decision-making habits and how to make the best decisions for ourselves, combining all of the knowing in our body. We'll practice connecting in a truer way with ourselves first and then finding our boundaries, empathy, and balance in our relationships. The chapter on learning gives us an insight into how we best learn, helping us to let go of self-limiting beliefs about our learning potential. Pondering on time and our individual rhythm of time shows us how we can live more within our rhythm, bringing ourselves closer to a peaceful state of mind.

In part three, we build up to identifying and owning all that we are passionate about and our individual gifts and values. This reveals or strengthens our life purpose. Standing strongly in who we are, we light up the path of our potential. Moving steadily in that direction, we trust and believe that the continued inspiration and support that we need in our chosen path will meet us along the way.

We ask ourselves the questions:

- If I took back control, what would I do in the world?
- What are my passions?
- What are the gifts I have which I can share with the world?
- What is my purpose?
- What empowers me?

Part Four - Healing Practices

The final part of *Divine Energy: Insight, Healing & Potential* includes key guided meditations and practices that will support you as you process each topic and give you strength and peace in your everyday life.

- *The Grounding Meditation* helps us realise the power of our words and be present in our power.
- *The Five Finger Breathing Technique* anchors our attention and helps us to focus.

- The Calm Breath gives us a sense of ownership of the space around our body which gives us relief from feeling all the emotions of people in our environment and brings peace to our minds.

- *The Rope of Life* is a powerful three-part healing meditation. Part one helps us process difficult experiences in our past. Part two brings us strongly into the present, and part three helps us let go of negative influences as we plan and own our future, such as self-sabotaging thoughts.

- *The Bubble Meditation* can promote a feeling of protection, and practising it helps us become more aware of the frequency of our energy as it flows through us.

- *The Healing Meditation for our Bones* highlights our skeletal structure and the trauma, shock, stress, tiredness, and negativity it has absorbed. We bring comfort, ease, and vitality to our bones.

- *The Loving Heart Meditation* supports us in honouring, soothing, and healing the hurt, sadness, shock, and emotion stored in our hearts.

- *The Healing Lungs Meditation* helps us as we breathe to exchange the resentment, suffocation, grief, and sadness we have held onto in our lungs for love, light and healing.

- *Deep Meditation* is a beautiful restorative practice that helps us to reflect, relax and replenish our energy.

Part One

Understanding Who You Are

Chapter 1

The Four Key Elements

Self-awareness involves creating the habit of regularly checking in with ourselves and observing our internal world; what we are thinking, how we are feeling physically and emotionally, the pace and depth of our breathing, and observing what person or situation has our attention. We feel good when we have a clear mind, feel at ease in our bodies, experience positive emotions such as love, joy, and connection, and choose where to focus our attention.

Four key elements give us a way into this state of feeling good and access to our personal power and potential. They are: taking back our control, trusting ourselves, believing in ourselves and having faith in a higher and loving consciousness. These elements are the cornerstones of our healing through self-awareness and self-development. We will explore each one in turn, then, as you read your way through the book, frequently check-in and be aware of how each element is developing within you. When we recognise and develop our control, trust, belief, and faith, we live from our true and real selves. We feel plugged into the energy of life, brimming with ideas, and confident in our ability to follow our passions and deal with whatever comes our way.

Control

I have lost myself trying to be what everyone wants me to be.
Now, I am letting go of everyone as I am accepting myself for who I am.
Having control means having the decision-making power in our own life. When we have control, we are the one who decides on the direction our life will take in the present and future.

When we are babies, our parents or guardians hold our control as they look after and teach us. They make decisions for us as they see best such as feeding us, helping us settle for sleep, and structuring our day. Gradually, as we grow, our parents relinquish that control, and we begin to make more decisions for ourselves. We find our own interests, goals, purpose, and outlook on life. Through our teens and into adult life, they continue to keep some of our control by creating boundaries that allow us to grow into taking responsibility for ourselves gradually. This gradual release of control as we grow and mature with life experience is the ideal way to learn. Upon reaching adulthood, it is important to, respectfully, take back our control, so we have the power to make our own decisions and divert our actions towards achieving our goals. It is good to be aware of how much control you give away to your parents. I have worked with some older adults who, without realising it, had never taken theirs back even though their parents are now deceased. They were still making all their important life decisions thinking about what their mother or father would have expected them to do. Fortunately, it is never too late to take back our control. We can do this simply by declaring to ourselves that we will live our own lives and stop deferring to others and allowing them to take our power. As we do this, we learn our self-worth does not have to depend upon fulfilling other people's expectations.

Sometimes it is to a friend, teacher, lecturer, boss, or partner that we give away our control. This person may dominate conversations, push their opinions on us, undermine our thoughts and effort, prevent us from having the experience of our own opinions, and overwhelm us with their judgement, manipulation, or perceived superiority. It can feel like someone has forcibly flooded your head with their ideas, information, and expectations, leaving your body with no room to feel like yourself. This is particularly difficult in long term relationships. Being on the receiving end of continuous controlling behaviour is very draining as it erodes your self-esteem and sense of identity, making taking back your control more difficult. Seeking help from a counsellor or support group can give people the starting boost needed to regain their power.

When we do not have our own control, it's possible we may attempt to take control of other people's lives and situations. Once we realise this, we can let go of our grip and address the cause of our need for people and situations to be a certain way.

Some people may subconsciously choose to give away their control so they can avoid being responsible for themselves or so that they can fit in a friend group, which can result in them blaming or resenting others for how things turn out for them. Giving away our control can result in paying the price of giving away a high percentage of our life-force to other people, which lessens our ability to cope with daily life.

Keeping our control is an ongoing learning process throughout life. There will be times when it will be more challenging, such as when we experience grief, loss, or change. But taking back your control is about making personal boundaries and honouring your own needs. It is about letting go of constantly needing approval. It is about developing the confidence to choose a direction for yourself and communicate your decisions with respect. It is the exciting journey of learning to live your own life.

Ask yourself to whom and to what situations do you give away your control, and then make a decision to stop giving away your power and, from now on to bring your own thoughts and feelings to the fore as you move forward in your life.

Trust

I trust my gut feeling, my intuition of self.

Trust is a willingness to follow our gut instinct and our feelings without over analysing thoughts. It is about being brave enough to look at how we honestly feel about situations. Trusting yourself involves knowing the goodness inside you and the value of your intuition. Our trust in ourselves can be diminished when our trust in others has been betrayed. For example, a significant adult in our childhood let us down; our partner withheld substantial information from us; a friend shared something we confided in them with others; or an upsetting event occurs such as a burglary. When such knocks rattle our trust, we can take some quiet time to check in with ourselves and revalidate our self-worth.

Through meditations such as the ones in this book, we can release hurt and disappointment from our bodies. We can learn from our past experiences to acknowledge the gut feelings that emerged when we knew things were not right. We can heighten the importance of our intuition and learn to fine-tune the balance between protecting ourselves and opening ourselves up to new experiences and challenges.

To observe how much you trust yourself, think about the last time you made an important decision, such as applying for a new job, making travel plans or starting a course. Did you think about it excessively and ask many people what they thought you should do? Or did you quieten your thoughts, clear all the information from others out of your mind and ask yourself how you actually felt about the situation? When we look for an opinion from other people, we give part of our trust to them because we allow their opinions to influence us. Advice can be useful, but it is only when we have full trust within ourselves that we can make the correct decisions. Sit quietly and imagine the various options you are considering as paths you could take. Practice connecting your gut to your mind's eye and see which path feels the best way forward for you. When we do this, we are owning our intuition and making the right choices for our life. A sense of trust in yourself leads you to being able to trust others. Things have a way of working out for you when you trust in yourself. Your true instincts will always serve you well.

Belief

The best is yet to come. You can do this. Be one with yourself.
You are powerful.

Self-belief is a self-built key element of our personal power and potential. Each brick of this cornerstone is made with a decision, a decision to accept our own inherent value, to accept the permanent worth that is yours, a firm decision that you are deserving of love and happiness, a decision that you are going to achieve the success you desire and a decision to be compassionate with yourself yet undeterred in your chosen direction. Belief is about knowing that despite your current life circumstances, you are the creator of your future.

We often underestimate the power of our will. However, when we look at the people we admire, they have all made determined decisions to live their life based on certain values, such as kindness, patience, honesty, creativity, adventure, and to pursue a particular dream or way of life. The consistency of their belief in themselves leads them to achieving their goals. Using this as your inspiration, build a foundational structure for yourself to believe in and then allow it to evolve with life experience.

To make or upgrade your structure, ask yourself:

Who am I?
What am I passionate about?

What do I love to do?
Who do I admire?
What do I want to achieve for myself?
What do I value?
What am I good at?
What do I want to share with others?
What do I want to learn?
What skills would I like to develop?

Build a belief structure for yourself out of everything you value. Know that you are worthy of this because you believe in it. A strong belief in yourself and what is profoundly important to you gives you strength, confidence, resilience, good decision-making skills, and a direction in your life. When you have your control, trust in your gut, and believe in yourself, you have the fuel to make a good life for yourself. Having a strong faith gives your life a whole added dimension.

Faith

Faith is our spiritual connection with a loving and higher consciousness. It is about expanding our trust in ourselves out into the great unknown and trusting that there is a force there, a superior awareness, that loves and supports us and who is deeply connected to who we really are. Developing our faith means opening our hearts to the solutions to problems, support in difficult times and guidance from a higher wisdom. Religious beliefs may contribute to our faith but having faith is not about following a particular religion. Ask yourself what works for you. Faith is a source of inspiration, knowledge, and wisdom. Having faith includes being able to connect the presence of who you are as an individual person, to your gifts, purpose, and goals in life, to the divinity in yourself. When we do this, we can invoke a sense of calm and peace. Faith gives us the grace to cope with difficult times in our lives because we have a sense that underneath what is going on, everything is ok because it is part of our learning and life lessons.

Faith helps us to notice the different ways in which support and love come to us. It gives us access to a power that helps us learn, create, and feel our oneness with the world. When you have your control, trust and belief within yourself, faith gives you an abundance of life-force energy to help you live in the fullness of yourself.

My personal faith has developed since childhood when I had a strong belief in God and Mary's kind, loving support. It was a typical Irish faith that expanded with the experiences of my gift of sight, of knowing, and of healing. I can feel and see the spiritual dimension of life, the holiness in myself and others. I am distinctly aware of my spiritual guides, who are my family members who have passed, mentors and superior guides who teach and support me and share information and love for the benefit of others. When I tune into my spiritual connection, I have a feeling of moving up into an expanded and higher consciousness. I resonate with the whole of my being and have a profound sense of being at home. A feeling of peace and joy flows into my heart and body. I feel present in the light that is the source of everything. I am one with this source energy, loved unconditionally.

Taking the time to quieten our minds through meditation, breath work, and yoga gives us access to experiencing this beautiful feeling of well-being. We can rekindle our connection and draw this divine source of strength and grace down into our daily lives in this space.

> *Journal Exercises*
>
> *Who has your control?*
>
> *From whom do you need to take your control back?*
>
> *Do you trust your intuition?*
>
> *Do you value other people's ideas and opinions far above your own?*
>
> *Do you know your own value and worth?*
>
> *What do you believe in that gives you a sense of your goodness and strength?*
>
> *What do you value? For example: kindness, honesty, fairness, love for self, family and friends, curiosity, respect, gratitude, courage, forgiveness, perseverance.*
>
> *What is your faith?*
>
> *What do you feel connected to that gives you hope, gives you power to achieve your goals, and sustains you in difficult times?*

Stepping Back -A Time When Hazel Took Back Control

Standing in a clothes shop when my marriage had just ended, I found myself completely unable to choose an outfit. I stood bewildered, looking at rails of clothes, asking myself, "What sort of clothes do I even like? What should I try on, let alone buy?" I was stuck deciding on one dress over another, the thin stripe or the floral? It suddenly hit me as though every dress suddenly dropped off its hanger to the floor. I didn't know what I liked. The mannequins watched me in their perfectly acquired outfit and matching accessories. This should not be so hard.

I was so used to making decisions based on the expectations of others - my parents' and then my husband's. I felt like an empty shell as I looked over the rail of colourful fresh dresses. But as the colours, styles, and choices bombarded me, I realised it was time to be my own person and not hide under the choices of others. I felt so overwhelmed. I took a deep breath, inhaling the calm to focus my mind and breathing through the urge to ring my sister to come and help me decide. You see, I had been so consumed for such a long time by the decisions and thoughts of others. I didn't have the control and trust that I could be my own person and live as myself. Instead, I became what everyone else around me needed and wanted.

For too long in my life, I didn't have my own mind. So I took on the role of soothing my father's anger and my mother's upset and worries. I got into the habit of letting others speak first and went wherever they went and needed me to go. With simple steps like buying the clothes I love, listening to music I enjoy, and discovering the things in life I genuinely like, I became my real self. After this awakening, over the course of the next year, I settled into my true personality. I rediscovered my strength, my kindness, my listening skills, and my sense of humour. I felt a new sense of contentment and purpose. I learnt to speak my truth in a calm, direct way. And I chose the floral dress.

My Mother's Faith

In her later years, my mother developed a severe and chronic ulcer in her lower leg. It was so painful and deep, covering half of her right calf. A nurse came every second day to dress the open wound, but it showed no sign of improvement, and the medical prognosis was that it was going to take at least a year for it to heal, which was very distressing.

One afternoon Mum was telling me about the pain she was in and wondering how she would endure it in the long term. I looked at her searchingly and asked her if she still had her faith. My mother answered immediately that she did. We made a pact to believe that her leg would heal quickly and completely. I worked on it every second day with healing energy. In a mere three months, her leg was perfectly better. The results of our combined faith amazed us both and the nurse.

The Four Key Elements: Key Points to Remember

- Taking back your control gives you the power to make your own choices and decisions.
- When you trust your intuition you make the best decisions which give you the best outcomes.
- When you decide on what it is that you value and believe in yourself, you develop the confidence and resilience to achieve your potential.
- Developing your faith gives you access to an infinite source of love, strength, hope, peace, and wisdom.

Chapter Two

Life-Force Energy

Life-force energy is the stream of aliveness and presence that runs through our physical body, sustaining our lives. It creates a magnetic field of energy around us that holds all the information of our life, including our physical health and our emotional, mental, and spiritual well-being. When our life-force energy flows well, we feel good, physically, emotionally, mentally, and spiritually. The energy that runs through us has a vibration. I visualise it flowing in waves through the body with a gentle hum.

To understand energy more fully, think of someone you know whose life-force energy is very strong and vibrant. This person is enthusiastic, positive, authentic, passionate and kind. It is a joy to be in their presence, and their vibrancy is contagious. They recover quickly from setbacks. Now think of someone whose life-force energy is currently low. They may be fearful. Their thoughts can be quite negative. After spending time with them, you feel tired and drained. If their life-force has been low for a long time, they may be in pain or suffer from chronic illness.

If the concept of energy flow in the body is new to you, try feeling the sensation of energy by holding out your hands, palms facing, close but not touching. Hold the intention in your mind of feeling the sensation of an energy flow between your hands. Experiment with a sense of fun. With palms still facing, slowly move one hand up and down above the other. Swap letting the opposite hand move. Notice sensations of tingling, pressure, heat, cold etc. Next, hold your hands a little apart and imagine making a ball of energy between your hands. Gently pulsate your hands a little in and out to allow you to feel the sensation of the energy ball as it builds. Repeated practice increases the energy flow.

To increase the vibrancy of your life-force energy, do the following exercise regularly.

Bringing Up Your Energy

We are energy, and without energy, there is no life.

The following method of "bringing up your energy" is a powerful and fast way to elevate your energy levels and flood your body and mind with positivity and strength. Increasing the energy flow in the body brings oxygen to the brain, lifts our mood, and promotes healing and well-being.

It is important for us to spend some time every day in a relaxed state. Our minds need a chance to slow down, allowing our thoughts to settle. Our muscles need to relax and let go of being constantly braced for action, allowing the skeleton to realign and our circulation to flow more freely. Our nervous system needs soothing and time off from being on high alert. Practising relaxation exercises such as this one will improve your physical, emotional, and mental well-being.

If you set aside 20 minutes, three times a week, for such relaxation exercises, you will feel a remarkable improvement in your physical, emotional, and mental state in just three weeks. During the day, if you feel stressed simply, take a deep breath, imagine your life-force becoming brighter and stronger and let the tension go.

You may find it helpful to choose a colour for the energy and imagine being filled with this colour as the energy flows through your body. If you find it difficult to empty your mind, at the end of this exercise, just allow thoughts to flow in and out of your mind and observe them without focusing on any particular one.

- Sit in a chair or lie on your back with your feet shoulder-width apart.

- Relax your pelvis, hips, stomach, chest, shoulders, throat, and neck.

- Feel the sensations in your body, your life-force energy. When you are stressed or anxious, your life-force is weakened, and when you relax, your life-force becomes stronger and brighter.

- Imagine your life-force coming in through your feet, legs, hips, stomach, chest, neck, back, and head and out through the top of your head. Next, visualise it circling back again into the feet, up through the body and out your head. Allow this cycle to continue without your conscious thought.

- Take back your control, trust in self, self-belief, and faith in your potential and in the support that is there for you.

- Inhale slowly through your nose, completely filling your lungs holding your breath for three seconds. Next, exhale slowly through your nose or mouth, completely emptying your lungs until you feel it in the bottom of your stomach. Repeat this three times.

- This will slow everything down. Bring your breathing in line with the rhythm of your heart.

- Clear your thoughts. Empty your mind. If you find this tricky initially, just let go of analysing your thoughts. Allow them to flow in and out, passing through your mind.

- Breathe even more deeply and slowly, focusing down into your feet, feeling the life-force energy going up through your feet, through your calf muscles and into your knees. Let the energy flow into your thighs and hips, relaxing the muscle.

- Allow the flow to continue into your pelvis. Imagine holding the energy here for four seconds and then release it and allow it to flow from your left to right hip.

- Let the life-force energy flow from your pelvic area into your stomach, relaxing the muscle in this area.

- Let it flow from your stomach into your breastbone (this is where we hold suppressed emotions), hold the energy here for four seconds, release your emotions, and relax all the muscles in this area.

- Focus back down on the tailbone bringing energy into this area for ten seconds. Then, let it flow up along each disc in your back, into the lungs and the back of the lungs, shoulders, neck, and head, relaxing all the muscles.

- Focus back to the breastbone, putting more energy in again for four seconds, letting it flow into the chest and around the heart area. Imagine heat building around the heart and through the back of the heart, relaxing the muscles.

- Focus now into the throat area, feeling your life-force energy build here for four seconds, let it flow up into the face and head, holding it inside your head for ten seconds. Let it flow up and out through the top of your head.

- Now imagine a ball of white healing light coming into the bottom of your spine. Hold it here and let the power of it build-up for 10 - 20 seconds. Next, imagine heat in this area and then let it travel up through your spine along each disc, feeling it pulling you together, making you strong.

- Feel your connection to the earth through your feet, allowing you to feel grounded and strong. Visualise a peaceful, protected space all around your body. Your breath flows with more ease. Your mind feels quieter. Your stomach is more relaxed. Your heart feels settled. You feel connected with your whole body.

Stepping Back

This exercise was particularly useful to me in recent years as I held onto and manifested my dream of buying my own house. Once my relationship ended, I started renting accommodation. Most renting arrangements were short-term, and every year or so, I'd find myself in the position of having to move again as landlords sold their properties or moved back in themselves. The cost of renting was steadily rising. Every time I'd catch myself feeling down as I packed up all my belongings, I'd bring up my energy to feel strong and change my perspective so that I could cope with another move and not be overwhelmed by it. I'd bolster my belief that in the near future, I'd be turning the key, opening the front door of my very own house. I'd revel in the feeling of the excitement of this future. Before she passed, I'd frequently chat to my mum about my plans and soak up her encouragement.

The journey to owning a house gave me lots of practice in bringing up my energy. The banks were not eager to provide a mortgage for a self-employed holistic therapist approaching fifty with no pension. Luckily my local credit union started giving out larger long-term loans and agreed to lend me the money I needed. I found a house I liked, but there were issues with the current ownership that resulted in the sale falling through and the loss of my deposit. It was a tough blow, but I'd quickly go up in energy every time I felt negativity creeping in. I'd think to myself, "this is not as bad as it initially looks." I'd chat to myself in a positive, logical way. Emotional support and the physical help to move again to new rented accommodation came from my family, helping me to trust that everything would work out.

And then a little synchronicity came into my life, leading me to standing outside what was to be my lovely little house and agreeing on a price the day before it was to go on the market. A few months later, I received the long-awaited phone call that the sale had fully gone through, and the keys were mine. As I jumped and danced about with absolute elation, a butterfly came in the open window and fluttered all around me. I felt my mother's love and joy that this moment was happening for me. Bringing up my energy had led me on the steady (albeit slightly longer than I had anticipated) course to a done deal.

Life-Force Energy: Key Points to Remember

- You have life-force energy which flows in, through, and around your physical body.

- When the flow of this energy is strong you feel good physically and emotionally.

- When the energy is not flowing well you may feel negative, tired, anxious, or in pain.

- You can practice the "Bringing up your energy" exercise and bring ease into the body and a feeling of strength and well-being.

Chapter Three
Sensitivity, Intuition & Listening

We all have a different level of sensitivity. Our unique perception of the same set of circumstances affects each of us in different ways. Certain smells, noises, tastes, and textures are enjoyed or disliked by different people. What hurts, embarrasses, offends, upsets, or troubles one person might not bother another. What is noticed and deeply felt by one person, someone else might not even see. We need to honour our level of sensitivity and be aware that it is something that changes as we go through our teenage years and our adult life.

Our level of sensitivity tunes us into our intuition. You may be very in tune with what others around you are thinking and feeling. This can make you an empathic listener, someone who listens to the words being said and also to the feelings and thoughts behind the words. However, it can also make busy environments such as school, work, and family gatherings overwhelming at times.

When we are intuitive, we sometimes listen to someone telling us about a situation and feel very confused. This is because we know what they are saying doesn't fit properly with the emotions they are displaying. The story doesn't feel complete. They have possibly learned to hide behind personalities they have created or raised barriers and are not showing their true selves. Understanding this gives an intuitive person clarity and helps them separate themselves from the other person's drama.

During and after busy situations or difficult conversations, we need to learn to trust our intuition and gut feelings to see things clearly, to become aware of when others are being forceful with their energy, and the feeling of someone pulling or draining your energy. Try not to question and analyse yourself. Instead, trust your gut and take care of yourself by separating your thoughts, feelings, and opinions from the people around you. Think about what is their information and what is your own. Take back your control and your ability to make your own decisions. Take back your trust in yourself and your own intuition. Take back your self-belief. Think, "I am separating myself from you, giving back what doesn't belong to me, and being true to myself." Ground yourself by becoming aware of your connection to the earth through your feet. Visualise strength flowing into your spine. Imagine creating a space of protection for yourself 360 degrees around your body. As your thoughts clear, you see things accurately. You can manage your own emotions. You can step back into your own power. You no longer feel overwhelmed.

Valuing your sensitivity means acknowledging what you can sense from others while also staying centred in your own power and your own identity. With practice, sensitivity becomes a very powerful gift to the world. As we learn to read people, we gain a deeper understanding of their words and actions. We have compassion for where people are at and can see the best in them. We give good advice when asked because we sense the impact of people's past and personality in their present situation.

The Calm Breath

Be patient with yourself and others. Find the inner calm within you. Trust it.

The Calm Breath helps you create space around you so that you can be yourself, feel your own power, and feel protected from being overwhelmed by the thoughts and emotions of others around you. It is done at a moderate pace using some force with the out-breath.

With frequent practice of the calm breath, you will notice that people and situations which used to make you worried, angry, impatient, upset, or anxious do not have the same impact on you. As a result, you can go about your day with a sense of calm.

- Imagine there is a membrane surrounding your body that contains your life-force energy. It is quite close to your body.

- Breathe in a deep breath through your nose for a count of 3. Then, breathe out through the mouth for a count of 5, pushing the membrane a little bit away from your body, 360 degrees around you.

- Feel a sense of space and stillness around you for a moment.

- Breathe in again for a count of 3. Then, breathe out for the count of 5, expanding the space all around you. Pause to feel the space and stillness for a moment.

- Do this several times until you feel your body relaxing, making sure after the out-breaths to sweep the calm feeling all around your body.

- Feel how you have changed the energy and atmosphere around you.

- Feel inside your feet and your connection with the earth to ground yourself.

- Feel your own power and how clearly you can see what is going on in the present moment. Notice how much quieter your mind has become.

- Feel your access to your logic and reasoning as you sit or stand calmly in your space.

> ***Journal Exercises***
>
> *Sensitivity*
>
> *How sensitive are you?*
>
> *Do you often tune into other people's emotions and pain?*
>
> *Do you find it hard to make decisions in your life because you question yourself so much?*
>
> *Do you tend to over-analyse what other people say and do?*
>
> *Do ou find it hard to differentiate between your intuition and other people's input? (When you tune fully into your gut and intuition you get a solid answer, it feels right. It's an inner knowing like an instinct. If the information comes from someone else it stays in your head and you analyse it.)*
>
> *Do you find it difficult to brush emotions away unless you fully understand the dynamic of a situation?*
>
> *Which environments, situations and people drain your energy and make you feel tired?*
>
> *Which activities, environments, and people help you to restore your energy and give you a sense of well-being?*

Listening

Our sensitivity and how we manage it is closely linked with the quality of our listening skills. Good listening is so much more than just hearing words. It involves reading body language, the subtle movements people make, being aware of the tone of voice, the emotions expressed through different amounts of emphasis placed on phrases and words, and feeling the vibes of conversations and situations. The more comfortable we are with being present in the moment and in tune with our senses, the greater our ability to listen. We are open to the information being expressed and can hear what is being said with clarity. We can be there for someone when they really need understanding. When we are tuned into sensitivity, we are better able to choose the right person to confide in or the best time to speak when we have something we want to say. It is a wonderful gift to be truly listened to. It helps us feel valued and compassionate towards ourselves when we are going through a tough time. Listening is a two-way thing. When two people are still and peaceful in themselves and focused only on what one of them is expressing, there is a whole new quality to the communication, which is enriching and empowering for both.

Sometimes we can unconsciously be poor listeners. This can especially happen during times of change such as puberty when hormones heighten our awareness to the point of overwhelming us, causing us to close ourselves off from fully witnessing the present. However, we can remedy this once we become aware of our listening habits. To identify yours, ask yourself questions such as the ones in the following journal exercise section.

Journal Exercises

Listening

Are you in the present when someone is speaking to you or lost in thoughts about the past or future?

Do you remember what someone has said, or do you let the words flow by without processing the conversation?

Are you good at deciphering what is real and not real when someone is speaking, knowing what is true and what is untrue, or an exaggeration, or drama? Do you put your own slant on what someone is saying to suit your own agenda?

Are you dismissive of someone when they start to talk, predicting what they are going to say, shutting down, and cutting off the line of communication?

Do you interrupt people not allowing them to finish their information which they needed to express and instead jump into talking about your own experience or opinions?

Do you change the topic when you don't want to hear what someone has to say?

Do you tend to joke your way out of serious conversations and cause the other person to lose their train of thought?

Do you try to make someone say what you want to hear?

Can you protect yourself in conversations if someone is being too forceful, negative, or aggressive by calmly being assertive, walking away or using the calm breath to create your own space?

Do you make excuses for partners or friends when they don't listen to you?

What do you need to do to experience being listened to more fully?

How to Be a Good Listener

- Keep your attention in the here and now when someone is talking to you. Avoid allowing your attention to drift.

- Consciously take your place in the conversation as a listener as well as a speaker. Avoid talking over people.

- Support the other person to express themselves fully.

- Value what the other person needs to say.

How To Be Listened To

- When we have something that we need to express, there is a lot we can do to make it easier for the listener to hear us fully.

- Be clear in your mind about what you want to say.

- Know that what you have to say is valuable and worth the time someone takes to listen. Breathe and keep as centred as you can so that you don't trigger the other person into mirroring your heightened emotions.

- When you are speaking, allow one stream of thought or information to go through your mind.

- Follow that stream of thought right through to the heart of the matter, stating what you need to say before going onto a different topic.

- Repeat your main point in a way that will be understood by the listener if needed.

- Speak with clarity, good eye contact, and at an unrushed pace.

- Allow the other person time to give you their response.

- Trust your intuition on when to end a conversation. The person may need some time to process what you have said, and if so, it can be continued at another time.

The flow of conversation is engaging and productive when both sides are listening well. Ideas are brought forth and developed. Information is shared. People feel acknowledged and valued. Solutions are found. Compromises are made. Apologies are sincerely offered and accepted. There is a stream of aliveness in our communication.

A Memorable Writing Experience

We were brainstorming together to describe what it felt like to really listen, asking ourselves more questions than we were answering, and my guides told me to stop for a moment and that they'd show us, a space of peace and silence opened up around us in my sitting room. The room became completely still as we were taken into this space. For a couple of minutes, the noise of the day stopped, and we had no access to thought. We were in the moment, calm, peaceful, and so very present in a profound stillness. There was a feeling of awe and knowingness. This gift was sent to us so we could experience the state from which we can truly listen to ourselves or someone else with our whole being. The quality of that alive stillness stayed with us for some time.

Stepping Back - The Gift of Listening

I first learned about listening from watching my mother. She was affectionately called Ma Mooney by neighbours and friends who valued her ability to listen compassionately and give sound advice. She had developed a great strength because of all the challenges she had faced in her own life, such as the loss of her mother when she was only 12. She had been the youngest of five children then. Her father married again, and in time Mum had seven more siblings. My mother went on to have thirteen children of her own, and many of her siblings also had large families.

All of this life experience led her to be a woman that understood people. She'd notice when someone was out of sorts and say, "Come in and have an ould chat." Then I'd watch her, a cup of tea in one hand and cigarette in the other, settled in her chair, giving whoever was troubled the space to tell her what was going on in their lives and then what they needed to hear would just flow out of her mouth.

I remember, aged 13, mopping the kitchen floor, my angst in every swish of the mop. The tears were meeting under my chin, and a headache pounded behind my eyes. Mum said, "What's wrong, Hay? Come sit down!" I told her who had teased me, who had bossed me, who had tormented me over the last couple of days. Thirteen wasn't an easy age to be in the midst of so many siblings. When I got to the end of my woes, she helped me separate what made me feel so much turmoil. She chatted to me about the offending siblings' personalities and how I had let them press my buttons. She helped me see what I was adding to the situation and how I was gathering all of the upset in the house around me in a smothering way. She said, "It's no wonder that you have a headache!"

Mum told me what I should ignore from my brothers and sisters, to mind myself, and not get so upset. It continued to be somewhat of a challenge for me, but that headache eased, and it was a day that I felt particularly seen and understood by her. I miss being able to talk things through with her and feel her comforting advice.

Sensitivity and Listening: Key Points to Remember

- When we are unaware of our sensitivity we can be frequently overwhelmed.

- When we embrace our sensitivity we have the power of insight and clarity.

- Daily practice of the calm breath allows us to move through our day with a sense of calm.

- When we bring our awareness to listening and being listened to, the quality of our communication is significantly raised.

Chapter Four

The Power of Thinking

A thought is a mental object. It can be an idea or opinion produced by thinking. It can occur suddenly in the mind, either as a random bit of information or a flash of inspiration of your potential. Thoughts help us to understand ourselves and what is going on around us in the here and now. As babies, thinking involves our instincts and senses. As we move through childhood and into adulthood, thoughts involve language, life experience, and much more information. When a thought appears, and you give your attention to it, more thoughts like it start to flow through your mind. Thinking can involve observing, remembering, considering, analysing, studying, deciding, understanding, judging, obsessing, imagining, picturing, reflecting, and predicting. When we allow more than one stream of thought to be active in our minds at once, such as thinking about many topics at the same time, taking on others' opinions or worrying about the past or future, we overwhelm and stress our mind.

Everyone has their own way of thinking and processing thought. Our thoughts create our feelings, and the way in which we manage thoughts is what creates our life, our level of happiness, our ability to reach our potential, the quality of our relationships, our capacity to love, our ability to manifest our dreams, our openness, our physical health, our mental health, our resilience, and our ability to be fully present in the here and now. Looking at our thoughts, clearly seeing their effect on our lives and learning how to manage our thinking are essential life skills.

> *Your mind is a powerful tool. When you fill it with positive thoughts, your life will change. Believe in yourself.*

Processing Our Thoughts

People look at and handle their thoughts in different ways depending on their personality, life experience, and awareness of the impact their thinking habits have on them.

Thinking in a healthy and powerful way involves focusing on a thought and reading it through the body. This means connecting the thought to your feelings, your intuition, and naming where it impacts in the body to process it. What does the thought say to you? Take the information that is beneficial for you out of the thought. Then let the thought move on through your mind and out of your body.

Learning to process our thoughts properly, results in being able to manifest anything we want in our life. Our thoughts are powerful, providing us with a sense of our free will and the abundant choices available to us. They show us we can be strong and secure in our true identity and cope with and process anything that comes our way. By being present and clear in our mind, we can enjoy life's adventure to the full.

Freeing Up Space

Imagine your brain is like a phone in the way lots of information goes through it every day. Visualise it as a top of the range phone with huge capabilities. As you grow into adulthood, it updates and can do more and more complex things. You use it constantly. There's an app for each member of your family, for each of your friends, for all of the people you meet in your day, for your physical body including each of your senses, for all the thoughts you think, the positive ones and the negative ones, your feelings, your responsibilities, and your insecurities. There is an app for your workload or homework, projects, your worries, your past troubles and regrets, and your plans and dreams for the future. It takes in information from advertisements, YouTube, TV shows, and more. Messages and images from others are constantly coming in.

What we often do is leave most of the apps open at once. Some are constantly in use, and others run unseen in the background. Everything is activated. Nothing is fully resolved or closed down for a while. This quickly drains the power of your battery and often overwhelms the phone, causing it to freeze, malfunction, or demand memory to be freed up. To resolve this, you may need to restart your phone, charge it up, close down the apps. Next, you delete some unused apps or delete files that drain the phone's power and clog up its operating space. You may also decide not to ask your phone to cope with so many functions at the same time.

You need to learn to look after your brain in the same way, to learn to respect it and only to run the number of streams of information it can cope with at any given time. Your brain needs sleep to recharge and quiet time, so it can filter through and recover from the volume of information it deals with throughout a day. Your brain needs you to delete information no longer needed and for you to lessen the pressure under which you put it. You can then store information in its place, imagining what you have learned and experienced moving to the correct brain files. Next you can mentally hand information that belongs to others back to them. In this way, your brain becomes relaxed and functional. You feel good in yourself and can prioritise your needs, goals, and fun for the day and week ahead.

Storing Thought

Often we do not fully process our thoughts, which lead them to be stored in and around the body. We sometimes negatively add to these thoughts, replaying troublesome thoughts and events, adding our anxieties and fears to them. This distorts the thoughts. Truth and logic become warped, and clarity gets lost.

As a result, these thoughts become heavy, and pressure builds in our head. Our mind becomes overloaded. The thought can implode, breaking up into pieces and falling down into the body. The things we reflect on and contemplate can become stored in our muscles and organs, causing tension, disruption to blood flow in the body, physical discomfort, turmoil, and pain.

There are many ways we try to cope and manage with negative thoughts which are stored in the body, causing anxiety, stress, and tension. However, some of the ways we try to counter this turmoil result in even more tension and to us avoiding dealing with the core issue.

Floating
Floating is where we disconnect our attention from our body and float off. We distract ourselves from the issue at hand. By doing this, we may avoid feeling what's troubling us temporarily. However, the thoughts and feelings we ignore are still in the body and may be triggered back into our awareness by similar situations. Also, when we float away from our body, much of ourselves is not present in our lives, and we end up missing out on properly enjoying many worthwhile experiences.

Pushing out
Pushing out our thoughts is the manner by which we find the pressure of a thought in our mind overwhelming, and so we push the thoughts out. We allow them to float around

us, where there is more space believing this will allow us to look at them in a more manageable way. However, we may procrastinate about facing these thoughts. Pushing thoughts out will not help in the long term because the thoughts need to come back into the body and be connected with their corresponding feeling to be processed and moved through and out of the body to clear them properly. A jolt caused by an accident, injury, or emotional shock can result in an accumulation of pushed out thoughts suddenly rushing back into us needing to be faced.

How to Process Our Thoughts

When a thought or an accumulation of thoughts becomes distorted in whichever way, we must first pause our current thinking and take a couple of deep breaths. Start from where your thinking is at and then work in reverse to where it started. Sit and find the strong emotion at the root of where it began. Your thoughts will lead you back to that point. To do this, talk to yourself. Ask yourself questions. Answer each one, and follow its path, taking the distorted thought out of the body. Name the pain or pressure in the body by identifying and releasing the trapped emotion, allowing yourself to track back to the original thought to process it properly, release, and heal it. The following examples illustrate how to do this:

"I have a pain in my head. I feel annoyed. Why do I feel annoyed? Nothing has gone right all day since I felt upset this morning. I remember now what my sister said that upset me."

Follow this through by giving back the emotion which belonged to your sister in the comment she made. Feel the rest of the impact the comment had on you, breathe into it, and release the hurt from your body. Finally, soothe yourself with a positive thought and observe the headache easing.

"I feel overwhelmed. What's overwhelming me? I feel surrounded by racing thoughts, listing all the things that I have to do."

Breathe and feel the impact the chaotic way you are thinking is having on your body. Prioritise the job that really needs to be done and then line the other jobs up behind that one so you can deal with them in order, one at a time, in a more peaceful way.

"I feel pressure down my spine and a pain in the bottom of my back. What previous situation in my life does this feeling remind me of? It reminds me of that part-time job I had last summer, and I felt I couldn't get all the work done, and the manager spoke very angrily to me."

Bring up the feeling and thoughts which were held then. Give the manager back the anger and pressure he was passing on. Name and release the tough thoughts and feelings stored since then. Say kind things to yourself about the situation. For example, I am a good worker. I got on well with the customers.
After you work through processing your thoughts, go back to your current situation, and notice how it feels a bit lighter. Ask your thoughts to line up. Get a pen and paper. Bring through the thoughts into your body one at a time. Write down what you need to do. Discard any job that isn't necessary, release emotional baggage on any thought that belongs to others, and make a work schedule for yourself that includes breaks and is manageable. Focusing on one task at a time, start with the most important task. Acknowledge your skills and achievements as you work. Congratulate yourself as you finish each task and notice how well you can cope once you manage your thoughts in a better way.

Always start and end your day with a positive thought.
Positive thoughts and positive feelings will attract a positive life.

Dealing with Absent Thoughts

Absent thoughts are thoughts you didn't want to look at, so you stored them whole, deep in the back of your mind. You pushed these thoughts down so far that you couldn't see them, and they got lost and left your day-to-day thinking. We often do this with grief, loss, guilt, or trauma to avoid feeling the pain. However, you are still vaguely aware of the effort you use to keep these thoughts from emerging, which is draining your energy. You try to pretend that whatever upset you didn't happen.

Every so often, something happens to trigger one or more of these absent thoughts. Once triggered, an absent thought rushes in and presents itself. It can seem to have doubled in size with more power to upset you, and you feel you can't handle it. Be brave, breathe, sit, and acknowledge the memory. Remind yourself that it is the memory of an absent thought, and so, despite some strong feelings, it is not unfolding right now. Suspend your judgement. Bring up the strongest part of you. Talk to yourself at the age of the memory. You couldn't handle this situation very well when it happened, but now with life experience, you can see it in a different way. Be kind and reassuring to your younger self. Acknowledge the strength and wisdom you have since gained. Help your younger self see what happened with clarity and let go of the thoughts and emotions you kept suppressed.

Dealing with Panic Thoughts

Panic thoughts start with one thought that you analyse. You feel a jolt, and then a rush of thoughts follow. Fear-filled thoughts increase in speed. A panic feeling sweeps in quickly, making you feel overwhelmed. You want to dismiss the thoughts, but they keep coming in faster. The emotional impact hits you in the chest, heart, and lungs, and your stomach feels upset. You feel pressure on your head. Your heart speeds up and breathing becomes rapid and shallow.

You need to slow everything down. Breathe. Sit with it all and just feel for a few seconds. That is enough to stop the rush of thought and enable you to name the feeling behind the first thought that caused the panic. Think to yourself, "I'm alright." Use the calm breath to create space for yourself. You can handle everything more easily now. Imagine the word of the named feeling, behind the first thought, in 3D in front of you. In your mind's eye, see yourself walking around the word. Say reassuring things to yourself, taking the power out of the word. See it getting smaller and more manageable. Sit with yourself for a few moments and acknowledge the exercise you have done. Practice catching panic earlier and earlier so that you can slow your thoughts before they accelerate. With daily practice, you will learn to manage your panic.

Dealing with Scrambled Thoughts

Scrambled thoughts are thoughts you did not want to feel, so you stored the words of the thoughts and the corresponding feelings in different parts of your body. This can result in random feelings emerging that confuse you. You need to reunite each feeling with the words of the thought that created it so it can be processed and released. Use the calm breath to create some space around you. Take each feeling one at a time and place the word of the feeling in your mind's eye out in front of you. Ask yourself, "Why am I feeling this?" Trust the answer will come. Once you know why you are feeling this way, let it go. Repeat the process with each emerging feeling. Visualise powerful white healing light flowing through your mind and body. Ground yourself by focusing on the connection between your feet and the earth.

Journal Exercises

How much information do you try to hold in your head at one time?

Do you find it easy to focus and concentrate?

Do you experience memory loss?

Is your brain frequently over-thinking and over-analysing?

Do you often feel tired, stagnant, or overloaded?

What are you currently thinking about?

Are you thinking in a positive or negative way?

Are your thoughts about the present or are you generally thinking about your past or future?

Do you frequently allow your thoughts to accumulate?

What can you do to manage your thoughts in a better way?

Managing Thoughts: Key Points to Remember

- Create your space around yourself throughout your day. Imagine a soft boundary membrane around you. Make it a size you feel comfortable with and declare to yourself that the space inside is your space.

- Frequently say things to yourself during the day that soothe you.

- Include relaxing activities in your day that allow your thoughts to settle such as listening to music, playing football, drawing, or going for a walk.

- Take a few quiet minutes every day to mentally hand back to others their opinions and emotions that have impacted on you.

- Stop worrying. Be present in the moment and learn to trust in your ability to deal with things as they happen.

- Stay out of other people's drama, gossip, and arguments.

- Surround yourself with positive people.

- Deal with people, subjects, situations, and jobs one at a time.

- Loosely plan your day so that it has balance and a manageable number of tasks.

Chapter Five

Clearing the Impact of Others

Whether we are aware of it or not, we pick up on the emotions of others. We sense their physical pain and thoughts as we move through our day. The extent to which we do this and are aware of it depends on our sensitivity. For example, someone in bad form may throw a nasty comment your way, and you feel the impact of their anger in your heart or stomach. You may feel tired or have a headache after spending time with people who are negative. You may feel uncomfortable sitting near a certain group in a restaurant. You may pick up a physical pain while visiting with a family member who is ill. You might feel off-balance or overwhelmed after someone has tried to force their opinion or outlook on you. If your class or work colleagues are stressed, you may find your heart racing and your thoughts getting fearful. Your head might feel full of thoughts after a morning in town. You may feel unwell when a family member tells you about their difficult day in the evening. You may willingly be a listening ear for an upset friend but be unable to get their troubles out of your head and body long after your chat, replaying their troubles in your thoughts and feeling their emotional pain. You may feel upset after listening to the news.

We can often be unaware of the effect everyone is having on us and the impact we can sometimes have on others. Some of us are inclined to take on particular emotions such as worry, anger, sadness, and anxiety. Others are inclined to feel the impact of someone else's thoughts. There are those of us who sense and carry the physical pain of our loved ones. When you feel low or negative in yourself, you may accumulate more of other people's feelings, thoughts, and discomforts that resonate with your own.

Do not let other people and experiences have control over your emotions. You will find deep inner peace within yourself as you are.

Clearing the Impact of Others

By actively clearing the impact of the thoughts and emotions we absorb, we physically, emotionally, and mentally protect and strengthen our body. This gives us a greater understanding of who we are and what our true purpose is. The upsetting impact of other people's opinions, emotions, words, reactions, and physical pain will no longer stay in our bodies. By doing the following exercise, you will be much clearer in your thinking and feel happier and more energised at the end of your day.

Take some time in the evening to sit quietly and release the impact of others with this meditation:

- First, give yourself a moment to settle. Then, sit quietly and concentrate on how it feels inside your feet. Feel the life and strength in your feet, and allow this feeling to travel all the way up your body and out the top of your head.

- Take back your control and your self-belief. Feel the trust you have for your inner guidance. Acknowledge your faith and the support of others.

- In your mind's eye, imagine yourself in the here and now. This will keep you in the present as you learn to clear and understand yourself.

- Now imagine a ball of white light coming into the bottom of your spine. Hold it there and let it build for 5 – 10 seconds. Feel the heat, cold, or sensation in this area and then imagine the ball of light travelling up your spine along each disc, feeling it pulling you together.

- Now that you are in the present choose a person, situation, emotion, or physical pain that upsets you and repeats itself in your thoughts. What is it that you want to clear from your body?

- In your mind's eye, place that person, situation, pain, thought, or emotion in front of you. Feel or visualise what changes in you. What do you feel? Is it heaviness, lightness, pressure, tingling, sensations, heat, cold, or pain? Feel or visualise the impact that person, situation, pain, or emotion is having on you.

- Name the impact. Is it a physical pain? Is it an emotion such as annoyance, anger, sadness, anxiety, suffering, impatience, feeling overwhelmed, or something else? Is it an opinion, attitude, or stream of thought? Take a moment to name the pain, feeling, or thoughts you have taken on. Then, acknowledge what consumes you and who it really belongs to. For example, the headache from a friend's worry, the sensation in your chest from the anger of the shop assistant, the racing thoughts from the opinions of a work colleague, or the tiredness from the busyness of the shopping centre.

- Say to yourself, "I am separating myself from you and letting go of what does not belong to me." Now let go of the person, situation, pain, thought, or emotion. Let it go by simply saying it. As you release and give back what wasn't yours to carry, you will feel relief and a sense of lightness in your body.

- Do not question or analyse it further. Just let it go. Allow this situation, feeling or person to leave your body, physically, mentally, and emotionally. Feel the relief and ease in self.

- Choose a healing colour and visualise a ball of light of that colour moving into wherever your body needs it to go. Bring it in and allow it to be strong wherever it needs to be. Relax and tune into yourself.

- Be aware of what changes in your body, your thoughts, and your emotions. Welcome peace into your mind, love into your heart, and light and healing into your body.

- Now acknowledge your strengths. Choose one positive word to describe yourself and feel the quality of that word in your body. Own your strengths. Be aware of your own power and of how strong you are. Tune into your lower stomach, where your intuition and instinct reside and visualise bringing light and energy into this area.

- Visualise a pillar of white light in front of you, behind you, each side of you, above and below you, expanding in through you and all around you, healing and protecting you. Relax and stay with this for a few moments.

- Visualise a beautiful beam of light coming up through your feet, legs, and stomach, touching every fibre, cell, and organ in your body, up through your chest, heart, throat and out through the top of your head.

- Feel clear. Be anchored and grounded in the present.

When the Impact Is Overwhelming

Some people gather and store a large quantity of other people's thoughts and feelings. They either aren't aware of the way in which this happens to them, or they are but don't take the time to clear themselves off every couple of days. They suddenly find they have a tangle of thoughts and a web of feelings to contend with. If this happens to you, you may find yourself irritable, teary, unable to focus, feeling vulnerable, angry, overwhelmed, anxious, or sick with a cold or flu and finding it difficult to cope with everyday tasks.

To clear the accumulation:

- First, sit and take a few deep breaths, bringing your attention into the moment.

- Then imagine yourself stepping out of your body and moving around to sit opposite yourself.

- From this perspective, look at what you have done to yourself by storing all you have sensed from other people.

- Give yourself a good talking to, pointing out all you have taken on that doesn't belong to you.

- Start to sort out where all this accumulation of thoughts and emotions came from. Think of others' thoughts, feelings, and pain as *their* information. It's not your information so let go of it. Imagine stepping back into yourself and following the above exercise, visualising giving back all you took on, back to whomever it belongs, your parents, partner, siblings and wider family, friends, teachers, work colleagues, boss, and crowds you've been in recently. Feel the relief as you let go of all that wasn't yours. Have a night's sleep or nap to complete your release and recovery.

- Commit to regularly clearing yourself and to managing your sensitivity.

When World Events are Overpowering

We are constantly reading about and looking at the problems of the world in newspapers, on our phones and TV. Thinking about climate change, displaced populations, wars, forest fires, violence, disease, racism, drug-related crime, poverty, and horrific historical events can take a big toll on us. We can become filled with fear, negativity, and a sense of powerlessness. If this happens to you, you need to take some time to help yourself come back into your power in the present.

The solution to every problem comes from a place of love and connection, so excessive worry on your part will not add anything positive to these situations. Sit and clear the impact of any world problems which you regularly worry about. Resolve to reduce the amount of news you ingest to a more manageable volume. It is not your job to sort out all of these problems.

When you feel more positive, make choices on what you are inspired to do to help the world and spread love and kindness in your day. It may be to improve the quality of the natural environment in your area, such as planting trees, helping a vulnerable person in your community, or being involved in a sponsored event for a charity you support. Also, be positive about new generations bringing in clear positive changes to benefit the world.

By frequently clearing yourself and shifting your perspective from fear into connection and presence, you have the power to come up with new ideas, which have a large and positive impact on the world. Act from your inspiration, not your fear.

> *Journal Exercises*
>
> *Who or what situation is filling up your thoughts?*
>
> *Where in your body does this impact? Do you feel it in your chest, back, head etc.?*
>
> *How does thinking about this person, group, or situation make you feel?*
>
> *Is what you are focusing on their information or your information?*
>
> *What do you need to do to resolve this? (Follow the steps for clearing yourself)*

Stepping Back

A number of years ago, a client came to me for help with a case of painful mouth ulcers. She had been suffering for a number of weeks. Medications prescribed had temporarily eased their severity but had failed to heal them fully, and she was in considerable discomfort. I was immediately aware of the sensitivity of this gentle lady. My intuition told me that the soreness in her mouth was not hers. I knew that she was carrying someone else's pain.

As we chatted, it unfolded that she was caring for her sister, who had advanced mouth cancer. Her sister was in a very negative and fearful state. My client felt very sorry for her and took on the responsibility of trying to help her sister cope better with her illness and encouraging her to take on a more constructive outlook as she dealt with the cancer treatment and her life circumstances. The strain of this responsibility was taking its toll physically on her in a way that mirrored her sister's illness. I softly explained that she couldn't change the negative way her sister was thinking and that once she accepted that, she would be able to let go of the mental and emotional weight of carrying that self-imposed task. Subsequently, her mouth ulcers quickly healed. The way our physical bodies show us what we need to be consciously aware of amazes me.

> **Clearing the Impact of Others: Key Points to Remember**
>
> - Every couple of days, or as needed, check in with yourself to see which thoughts, feelings, and aches are not actually yours and instead belong to the people and situations around you.
>
> - You can learn to clear the impact that people and circumstances have had on you and feel so much better physically, emotionally, and mentally.

Chapter Six

The Releasing Breath

In this chapter, we will look at our approach to our day and the work we have to do. Sometimes we can rush too much, or we can be disorganised and forgetful. We may be too easy-going at times, avoiding things that we need to do or conversely try to tightly control all the events of our day without any flexibility. All of these four ways of being hinder us from accomplishing what we hope to achieve in our day. Most people have the habit of entering into a particular one of these default modes regularly. However, you can probably recognise some of your past behaviour resonating in all four ways of being. The next time you find yourself in one of these modes, use the releasing breath to help you get back to working in an optimal way.

Rushing About

Do you sometimes rush? Do your thoughts move extremely fast? Do you feel very impatient with the speed at which you are able to get things done? When we rush, we forget to breathe properly. Our harsh judgement of ourselves and others builds and often overspills as angry thoughts or words. When this happens, we need to slow down the flow of our thoughts.

The Releasing Breath is a beneficial tool for any of us who rush, helping us to be present and get what needs to be done completed in a more relaxed way. Sit comfortably. Tune into the build-up of thought or emotion in the body that you wish to release. Follow this cycle of breathing:

- *Breathe in for a count of four.*
- *Hold the breath and feel what needs to be released.*
- *Breathe out for a count of four, releasing that feeling, thought, or situation from your solar plexus.*
- *Repeat six times.*
- *Sit with self. Become aware of your whole body. Relax your heart.*

When your breathing is regulated, follow the guide below to slow yourself down.

- Stop and sit with self. Begin to breathe in and out slowly until you feel a little more comfortable.
- Ask yourself, "What are my thoughts?" Are your thoughts, worries, judgements, and fearful thoughts about not being good enough? Are you thinking anxiously because this situation mirrors previous stressful situations? Acknowledge your answer and sit with it for a few moments.
- Ask yourself, "How am I feeling in my body?" Is there discomfort or pain in your body?
- Check-in with your solar plexus and then lower abdomen to sense your intuition. Why are you rushing?

- Tell yourself that you need to slow down, that it's ok not to be perfect, that it is unfair and self-sabotaging to expect yourself to get through an unreasonable amount of work in a day.

- Tell yourself that you can manage any task by tackling it one piece at a time. Take a few moments to reconnect with self. Release pressure put upon you by others. Release excessive expectations of self and others.

- Connect your thoughts with the rest of your body by talking to thoughts and feelings at the same time. You have let your thoughts run ahead of you, which put pressure on your body. Ask your thoughts to flow in sync with your body so that you can feel the power of your presence as you go through your day.

- Breathe calmly for five minutes.

Being Disorganised or Forgetful

Do you leave things down and forget where you've put them? Do you race back into the house in the morning searching for something you've suddenly remembered you need for your day? Do you let projects and tasks build up, so you have too many deadlines coming up, leading to feelings of panic? Are you disconnected from self and feel either behind or ahead of yourself in your day? The releasing breath can help us to put some structure into our day.

- Sit with self. Slow down your thoughts. Check-in with these thoughts, and the corresponding feelings in your body. Accept that you have let yourself get flooded with thoughts and feelings without giving yourself a hard time about it.

- Breathe and allow the spin you are in to slow down.

- Release your anxious or nervous thoughts. Release thoughts of "Poor me!" Release feelings of being overwhelmed. Release your agitation and negativity. Release the dizziness.

- Breathe slowly.

- Once your thoughts and feelings are more manageable, separate what needs to be done. Prioritise! Organise your workload and how you approach it.

- If you find this difficult, think of someone you know that is good at organising themselves and ask for some help. Then take back your control. You are not a victim of your day or your workload. Take charge. Plan how you will manage what you want to do. Start tasks early so you can break them into manageable sections, cope well with life, and still have time for fun.

Creating a Tightly Controlled Environment

Sometimes we need a lot of rigid structure in our life. Do you keep your room and belongings in a very tidy exact way? Do you have an inflexible routine? Have you detailed plans made for your day, week, month, and the year ahead? Do you need your family or friends to behave in certain ways? Do changes to this structure and these plans cause you to be stressed and irritable? Do you feel like everything falls away and you have nothing to hold onto if you lose this structure?

Daily practice of the releasing breath will allow you to release the pressure cooker feeling and fear that comes from living like this in your day. It helps us when we need to tightly control our environment and manage a potential short temper to enjoy life more.

- Sit with self and observe your thoughts. Your thoughts and feelings can change very suddenly when something unexpected happens to throw your day off course. Acknowledge your thoughts, the stress and anger that come up when you can't control a situation and how difficult it is for you when your structure is under threat.

- Learn to pause and breathe instead of snapping at someone. Release the overwhelming feelings and say calming things to yourself. Reassure yourself that you can always make a new plan around anything that happens.

Practising the releasing breath will allow you to cope better and help you to learn to enjoy life's moments, even the ones that happen outside of your planning and predictions!

An Easy-Going Life

Sometimes we can tend to plod along through life. Do you like to take an easy pace and keep things simple, deciding on very manageable ways to do things and sticking with that? Do you avoid people who challenge your comfort zone? Have you made a decision not to put too much effort into life? Do you generally deal with issues by avoiding those involved and hoping the issue will fizzle out? Do you take in small amounts of information and let most of it go over your head? When you get the whiff of change or chaos, do you check out emotionally and physically, so you don't have to cope with the challenge? Do you constantly look to your parents, siblings, or friends to mind you and smooth out difficulties in your life? Do you have great ideas and dreams for your future but rarely put in the effort or take the risk needed to fulfil your goals? Do you feel jealous of others who are living the life you would like?

The releasing breath helps those of us who are quite easy-going to achieve our goals. You can use the releasing breath to help you cope with taking a big step forward in your life.

- When you want to create something new in your life, sit with its vision and imagine pulling it closer to you.
- Breathe slowly and observe your thoughts and feelings.
- How do you feel when you imagine following your dreams and ideas? Do you feel stressed about being out of your comfort zone? Where do you feel it in your body?
- Try not to flee from your discomfort! Sit with it.
- Use the releasing breath to let go of the fear of the uncertainty of how you will reach your goal and the unease of moving out of your comfort zone.

Frequent use of the releasing breath will bolster your coping skills as you move forward in your life.

A Memorable Writing Experience

This was a really fun piece to write. The energy of the personalities that we chose to base this piece on came in and opened up for us so that we could feel the emotions of each type of person as our own and then easily describe their traits and the blocks that needed releasing for their lives to become more balanced and happier.

The Releasing Breath: Key Points to Remember

- When you find yourself rushing about, use the releasing breath to deepen and slow your breathing and your thoughts.

- When you are working in a disorganised way and find that you are forgetting and losing things use the releasing breath to let go of anxiety and agitation so that you can prioritise what you need to do and structure a plan of work accordingly.

- When you notice yourself being too tense and rigid in your plans use the releasing breath to let go of anger, irritation, and narrowed expectation so that you can bring in a softness around your plans and have a little room for flexibility and fun.

- When you become aware of your procrastination and feel resentful of what others have completed or achieved use the releasing breath to face and let go of discomfort so that when you meet challenges you are ready to take them on.

Chapter Seven
Balancing the Body

Being balanced means being stable and steady. You are solid in your foundation. When balanced, you feel grounded and have a cool head. You are unflappable and move with ease through your day. Your mind is clear, and you feel still and quiet. You know who you are and are happy within yourself. You feel comfortable in your body. You know everything is ok in the here and now. Being balanced protects your energy. You are in sync with yourself and are not upset or confused by people or situations in your life.

We can be knocked off balance by many life experiences and events such as unpleasant interactions with people, accidents, relationship break up, loss of a loved one, trauma or unrealistic expectations from ourselves, family, friends, or colleagues. When our sense of inner balance is compromised, the optimal energy flow in our body is affected.

The following exercise is very effective for nudging ourselves back into balance. This is because we generally store whatever knocks us off balance more on one side of our body, causing more of our life-force energy and presence to flow through the opposite side. By allowing energy to flow from the freer side to the more blocked side, we release what we have taken on, restoring our sense of being centred. For example, you may store unwanted responsibility in your right shoulder, unexpressed opinions in the left side of your throat, a hurtful comment in your right cheekbone, anger in your right jaw, old fears in your left kidney, or hardship in your right hip. Everyone's body is different, but we all have our unconscious habits for storing things we would rather avoid feeling.

Balancing the energy flow through your body is an excellent exercise to help maintain good physical and mental health.

Your strength is your calmness, in the clarity of your mind.
Strength comes from putting the negative aside without reacting.
Be positive, be calm, and find your place of balance.

How to Balance Your Body

- Tune into your body, imagining it divided in two, left and right.

- Start with your head. Feel or visualise the sensations in the left side of your head. Notice any tension, pressure, discomfort, or pain. Repeat for the right side of the head. Now relax and allow the sensations to flow and balance between the two sides of your head.

- Next, feel the sensations in your neck and throat. Focus on the left side of your neck and throat. Notice the sensations. Then tune into the right side of your neck and throat and feel this area. Compare the two sides and allow energy to flow, balancing the neck and throat.

- Bring your attention to the shoulders, arms, and hands. Tune into how it feels in your left shoulder, left arm, and left hand and then how it feels in your right shoulder, right arm, and right hand. Relax your shoulders and allow the sensations to flow and balance between the left and right shoulders, arms, and hands.

- Next, feel the sensations in your chest, heart, and lungs. Tune into the left side of the chest and heart and the left lung. Next, tune into how it feels in the right side of the chest and heart and the right lung. Breathe deeply and allow the energy to flow and balance both sides.

- Feel the sensations in your stomach and intestine. Tune into the left side of the stomach and intestine and then the right side. Compare both sides and then allow the energy to flow and balance.

- Tune into your pelvis and hips. Feel the sensations in the left side of your pelvis and your left hip and then the right side of your pelvis and your right hip. Compare both sides and then breathe and allow the energy to balance.

- Next, bring your attention to your legs. Feel the sensations in your left leg, knee, ankle, and foot. Stay with this for a few moments. Next, tune into how it feels in your right leg, knee, ankle, and foot. Breathe and relax, allowing the energy to flow between the two sides, bringing in a feeling of being balanced.

- Now imagine a ball of clear white energy coming into the bottom of your spine. Hold it there, letting it build for a few moments. Feel the heat in your lower back and let it travel up your spine, along each disc, feeling it pulling you together.

- Feel your body grounded. Anchor both feet evenly into the ground. Visualise white grounding energy coming up from the earth, in through your feet. Allow it to move slowly up through your body and out through the top of your head. Acknowledge a sense of balance and strength in your body.

A Strong Foundation

Our foundation is our strength and the structure of our whole being. It is made from our life experience and learning from conception up to this moment. Our parents may have given us a good start on making our foundation with their belief in us and their outlook and values. If not, we can still build a good solid foundation for ourselves.

Look at your beliefs, values, morals, strengths, and goals to help you create your own platform. To decide what to include in your foundation platform, ask yourself:

"From where do I draw my strength and power as I go through my day-to-day life?"

"What helps me to recover when I go through tough experiences?"

"What gives me the self-confidence to reach for my chosen career, relationships, successes, and goals?"

You can visualise standing on a platform that moves with you everywhere you go. Your power comes from this platform. With awareness, you can look at the bricks that make up your foundation. Which of these bricks do you stand on? Which bricks can you strengthen or add to your foundation?

Draw strength from your foundation, the base structure of who you are.

Next is an example of a foundation platform. Make your own personal one to organise the beliefs, values and strengths which make up who you are. Revise it as you gain new insights.

My attention is in the present moment.	I have my control. I take responsibility for myself.	I trust my gut feelings.
I am worthy of love.	I believe in myself.	There is a power that is greater than me that I am part of.
I have people in my life who love me.	I have talents that I can develop.	I am kind and generous.
Everything will be okay.	I can learn anything I want to.	I am who I am.
I am loved by _____, _____, _____ and _____	I love _____, _____, _____ and _____.	I am good at _____, _____ and _____.
I can recover from setbacks.	There are many ways to achieve what I want.	I can spend time on things I feel passionate about.
I am connected to myself and others.	I am connected to life and grounded in nature.	I can separate myself from others' thoughts and emotions.
I am flexible.	I can take the learning from my good and bad experiences and be strengthened by that.	I can live in the rhythm of my own time.
I can forgive myself and others.	I believe in my own goodness and the goodness of others.	I can regularly sit with suppressed emotions and let them go.

Divine Energy Insight, Healing and Potential

I can resolve negative thoughts.	I have valuable gifts to share with the world.	I can use my breath to help me deal with all situations.
From the larger perspective, everything is always ok.	I can achieve what I set my mind to.	Help is always available to me.
I can let go of worry.	I am connected to a pure and powerful force through my spiritual connection.	I know my life purpose or part of my life purpose.
My sense of humour helps me to cope with things.	I set my goals and know I can achieve them.	I am worthy of my goals.
I am confident.	I am secure.	I know how to soothe my difficult emotions.
I own my own place in the universe.	I am calmly and powerfully present in my own space.	I know how to replenish my energy.

Personal Journal

Draw out your own foundation platform. Include:

The names of people who support and love you.

Constructive beliefs which sustain you such as, "I am worthy of love. I can achieve my goal."

What you are passionate about, interested in, and good at.

The successes you cherish and the hardships you have overcome.

Your values such as, loyalty, forgiveness, learning.

Things that soothe you such as a hot chocolate or watching a good movie.

Your platform will change over time, so it is a good idea to revisit it and replace or add new bricks as you move through different life stages.

Balancing the Body: Key Points to Remember

- In a state of balance you feel present, calm, centred, clear-headed, and content.

- With awareness, you can observe where in your body you habitually store the impact of situations which knock you off balance.

- Restoring a feeling of balance and steadiness is a skill which can be practised, developed, and mastered.

Part Two

Looking at Yourself Honestly

Chapter One

The Value of Feelings and Learning to Manage our Feelings

Our bodies communicate with us through our feelings. Every thought or pattern of thinking we have has a corresponding feeling in the body. Feelings are waves of vibrations that run through us that we interpret as joy, sadness, anger, fear, disgust, anxiety, excitement, etc. These waves of emotion naturally keep flowing through us, being felt most keenly in the lower abdomen and stomach. I think of the stomach as the brain of our emotions because tuning into our stomachs gives us clarity on how we feel. Sayings in our everyday language such as feeling sick to the stomach, butterflies in my stomach, and getting knots in my stomach indicate that we instinctively know the stomach is the feelings centre of the body.

Depending on our sensitivity and life experiences, the intensity of our feelings is turned up to various volumes. They are amazing. We can soar with happiness, shake with fear, be buoyant with hope, and seethe with anger, all depending on how we think and how our bodies interpret what is happening around us. Being present in our feelings, fully feeling them and naming them allows those emotions to flow through us. Everyone has feelings that cause them difficulty, ones they do not want to feel because they view them as overwhelming or unacceptable. A difficult feeling may be anxiety, resentment, anger, jealousy, guilt, sadness, despair, inferiority, or embarrassment. Sometimes we refuse to feel these emotions, almost shutting down our energy flow through the stomach and storing the emotions in our bodies where we don't have to immediately feel them. This restriction and suppression results in tension in our muscles and reduced circulation, which adversely affects the whole body's well-being.

When we shut down the feelings we disprove of, we also shut down much of our capacity for joy, connection, excitement, and love. Know that it is okay to feel the full spectrum of emotions. Every feeling has value in the information it has for us. We need to change the question we ask ourselves when a difficult emotion arises from *How do I avoid feeling this?* to *What is this feeling telling me?*

Feelings alert us to what needs our attention. When we try to ignore them, we tend to attract more situations in our lives that trigger similar feelings. The weight of carrying them can turn into pain and illness. However, the rewards for being brave and allowing it to flow through us and accepting it, is a feeling of relief, liberation, true aliveness, better physical health, and ultimately our true natural state of joy. Also, when we allow our real feelings to flow, other people around us are more at ease because we are our true selves.

The following is a guide to help you cope with feelings that you find challenging and might rather hide or deny. A lot of strong feelings come up when old fears or patterns of negativity from the past are triggered by something in the present. Remember everything that you feel is ok.

A meditation for coping with feelings and allowing them to flow:

- Sit quietly in a comfortable place and breathe slow, deep breaths.

Divine Energy Insight, Healing and Potential

- Become more aware of your thoughts. Allow your attention to float off after these thoughts into the past or future. Be aware if you are distracted and not in the present moment. Bring your thoughts back into the here and now, into this moment.

- Feel yourself floating off again. Bring yourself back into your time, here and now, sensing life moment by moment.

- Feel your body in the chair. Feel yourself grounded.

- Ask yourself what is the most heightened uncomfortable feeling currently in your body? Then, feel it in your body. For example, you may feel pressure, pain, or discomfort.

- Stay with the discomfort in a caring, curious way.

- What feeling is there? Is it anxiety, annoyance, or hurt? Name it. Sit with it and look at the situation that comes up around it. It could be a worry in the present or a situation from the past which has triggered an old feeling. Is the feeling from a present situation, from the past, or a worry about the future? Once you have this figured out, start breathing into where it is held in your body.

- What thought comes to mind next? Follow that thought into where you feel it in your body. Listen for the next thought. Do this slowly. Breathe into it.

- Look at the impact these words have on you in your life, in the past, present, and future. Breathe into them to release them from your body.

- Visualise a white light above your head.

- Allow this to come down and filter through your body. Allow it to become stronger in the areas where you are feeling pressure, pain, or discomfort.

- Feel what changes in you.

- Bring positive words into your body such as love, compassion, gentleness, acceptance, fun, creativity, and peace of mind.

- Allow these words to change your feeling into a positive. Acknowledge what changes in you.

- Visualise life-force energy coming up from the earth into your feet and body, helping you to feel grounded, connected, protected and solid in yourself.

Be compassionate, working at your own pace. Deal with one feeling at a time. Regular use of this meditation helps us to thrive emotionally. We often underestimate our capacity to heal and to let go of that which holds us back.

Worry

Worry starts with a thought or an image. You have a worry thought or picture about a situation and take it into your head. Your brain starts over-analysing. The worry thought heightens. Similar thoughts join the original one. The more you feed it, the bigger the worry gets. The worry takes over your headspace. Your brain is inundated and is not coping. So it starts sending out signals through the body.

A nervous, anxious feeling moves into the body accumulating in different areas affecting muscle and circulation. (This is not always the case as some people shut down their feelings and have a numb sensation). You stop breathing properly. The breath quickens and becomes shallow or sharp. There is less oxygen supplied to the brain.

This puts pressure on the head and then on the neck and back and is, in turn, felt down through the body. The temperature of your body changes, and you feel hot or cold. Pain is heightened. You no longer feel present and may feel out of control.

To Resolve Worry

If you sit for a few moments, you can resolve this worry. First, you need to settle yourself a little. Bring your attention to your feet and ground yourself by visualising your connection with the earth. Next, calm the heart rate by breathing in deeply, holding the breath for three seconds and letting it go slowly. Do this six times. This helps to return your focus to the present, returning a good supply of oxygen to the body and releasing some tension or pain. Breathe in. On the out-breath, visualise creating some space around yourself. Now you have made some space between you and the worry, and you can look at it more objectively.

How are you experiencing the worry now? Where is your attention going with the worry, into your past or your future? What are you thinking? Accept your current thoughts. Know that you can change them to more positive thoughts once you acknowledge what you are feeling. What are you feeling? Where is the pressure of it held in your body? What is the feeling? Go within, be brave, feel where the worry has impacted, feel the tight stomach or the full head or neck pain, etc. Sit with it. Breathe into it and release the impact of worrying from your body. What were you thinking that caused this feeling? Start with the last worry and work backwards, reeling in the worried thoughts one by one, reasoning with each one and saying reassuring things to yourself. Put positive images in your head, visualising the worry being resolved. Stand in your own strength as you soothe each worry away.

This is an example of a little boy who got locked in a toilet while on a school tour. Here is the path of his worry. When he couldn't open the door lock, he thought, "I can't open the door. I can't get out. I'm stuck in here. No one will know where I am. No one will notice I'm missing. The bus will go home without me. I'm stuck in here forever." He needed to address his thoughts, starting at the end and working his way logically through each one.

I'm not stuck in here forever because my parents will come looking for me and get me out. The bus won't leave without me because my teacher will count us before we get on the bus and notice I am missing. My friends will also notice I'm missing if I don't come back soon. They will work out where I am and come and find me. I can shout for help. Someone will hear me and get help. I can try a couple of things when I'm waiting for help to come, like pushing or pulling the door while I try to release the lock. If I can't open the door, someone will help me or push the door in. I can picture getting out of here quite soon. I will definitely get out of here. I can breathe slowly to help me relax. I am brave. Everything will be okay. And it was, as his teacher had the door unlocked within two minutes.

The Image of Worry

Sometimes a worry can come as an image rather than words. For example, an upsetting scene on the news or in a film can repeat itself in your mind causing you distress. The key here is not trying to stop the image from popping into your head but instead to take the power out of the emotional blow that it hits you with when you think of it. To do this, you first need to acknowledge the distressing feeling that the image triggers in you. Is it loneliness, hopelessness, anxiety, guilt, or something else based on your life experiences? Once you have identified the feeling, ask yourself where in your body is this feeling stored. Take some deep breaths into this part of your body. Then continue your inquiry and ask what other situations in your life caused you to feel and store this emotion. Any information such as the age you were or the people involved will help. It doesn't have to be fully remembered. Then as you breathe into the situation, displace the distressing feeling with positive thoughts, images, and words.

For example, suppressed feelings of loneliness can be healed with the feelings of connection to whoever you feel loved by and with reassuring thoughts about being strong in yourself and connected to your own power. If the image pops back into your head on another occasion, be ready to counteract the worry with thoughts and feelings that reassure you and give you back a feeling of being secure within yourself.

An Ongoing Worry

Sometimes we can have ongoing worries like a serious illness, a family dispute or financial pressure. It can start with a sudden impact when you first learn the difficult news or have a traumatic experience. You need to give yourself time to process this impact before you start trying to cope with it. Decide to look after yourself while you recover from the shock. Then choose a time when you will sit down and start putting a structure in place to deal with the situation. Your thoughts can tend to race into wondering how you could cope with the worst-case scenario. You need to be mindful of your tendency to do this and bring yourself back to the present. You can learn to talk yourself out of worrying by reassuring yourself. You can change the worrisome thought to something more positive. You can change the core feelings by imputing positive thoughts and images. Say kind, positive things to yourself. Visualise putting that feeling or thought into your body.

Be gentle and encouraging. Be still within yourself. Imagine positive outcomes. Decide what support you need at this time and plan to seek this help. Feel your connection and power. Think, "I am strength, I am joy, I am love, I am calm." Feel your power rising within you. Release the intensity of the worry. Just let it go. Notice your muscles releasing and your heart rate settling. You can cope. Everything will be okay.

> *Journal Exercises*
>
> **Understanding Feelings**
>
> *What are your current feelings?*
>
> *What thoughts have created these feelings in your body?*
>
> *Where in your body do you physically feel difficult emotions the most? Do you get headaches, backache, tightness in your chest, etc.?*
>
> *What do you need to do to take care of this part of your body?*
>
> *What changes in your body when you acknowledge your feelings and follow the steps to process them?*
>
> **Managing Worry**
>
> *What do you worry about?*
>
> *Where do you hold the worry in your body?*
>
> *Where did this worry begin?*
>
> *Were you able to look at it in a constructive way?*

Managing Negative Obsessive Thoughts

Sometimes when our coping skills are overwhelmed, we subconsciously create negative obsessive thoughts. We keep circling the thought in our mind, which can be overwhelmed by anger, sadness, guilt, loneliness, grief, or unworthiness. As a result, we feel we can't cope.

If you have a negative obsessive thought, pause, give yourself a few seconds to breathe slowly and just be. Your body and head will start to calm down. Visualise yourself pushing the thought out from your body a little to create some space around yourself. Take a deep breath into your true self, connecting your thoughts to your body. Observe the thought and start to reason with it. Give the thought a good talking to. Talk to the thought from the part of yourself that is strong. Reason with it. Bring in your beliefs, morals, and constructive opinions. Resolve it with a positive outlook and trust that all is well.

If you still have difficulty letting go of the thought, pause. Are you stuck because you keep telling yourself that you shouldn't be thinking this way? Let go of this idea. Accept that this is your current thinking pattern. Accept it as your starting point for moving to how you want to feel.

Are you in a self-destructive mode, stubbornly holding onto a thought? Are you reluctant to face the origin of this thought pattern? Are you holding onto your thought because you want revenge? Do you want to be right and need someone else to be wrong? Are you catastrophising? Observe yourself. Look at what holding on to this thought is doing to you physically, emotionally, and mentally. Holding on to the thought is not worth it.

You will gain so much by resolving it. Look for the information in the thought. Be kind to yourself. Be compassionate. Trust in your ability to resolve the repeating thought. The reason for an obsessive thought is an overwhelming emotion. Your mind is trying to protect you from what you feel you can't cope with. The obsessive thought is preventing you from feeling the true emotion. However, naming and feeling the emotion is the way to stop obsessive thinking.

Be brave. Breathe. Be present. Be strong. What is the emotion behind your obsessive thought? Is it unworthiness, powerlessness, anger, shame, grief, judgement, insecurity, rejection, betrayal, loneliness, or something else? What word describes the feeling based on your life experience? Name the feeling. Take in this realisation. Now you have named the feeling that is causing your obsessive thought.

Imagine the word of your identified feeling in 3D. For example, if your word was worry, imagine it like this. Place the word out in front of you in your mind's eye, and then imagine yourself walking around it, observing the feeling. Stay with it, observing the feeling for a few moments. Breathe.

Now think or look with your mind's eye. Where in your body have you been storing this feeling? Breathe into this part of your body. Decide to release the feeling and, on the out-breath, let some of it go. Repeat this for a few more deep breaths. What would you say to yourself to change this word for you? For example, if the word is judgement you could say things to yourself that help you feel safe. Choose the positive opposite to your feeling to help you to change it: fear to safety; anxiety to peace of mind; confusion to clarity; bitterness to enthusiasm; darkness to light; rejection to acceptance; loneliness to belonging; being stuck to a feeling of movement; weakness to strength and backbone; worthlessness to appreciation; abandoned to adored; depressed to loving life; aggression to gentleness; shame to pride; emptiness to fulfilment; anger to affection; sadness to joy.

Look at your word again. Allow the word to be released from your body and see it change slowly to its positive. You will notice that you feel better. What feeling does your body need to complete the healing? Place your hand on your heart and breathe this positive feeling into your body.

Now see your strengths in your mind's eye, your gifts, and your hopes for yourself. Decide to value yourself. Build yourself up by talking yourself into a more positive outlook. Observe what you need to say to yourself to help you to feel better. Write out a positive thought for yourself on a card, an affirmation of your strengths and wellbeing so you can remember to say it to yourself, repeatedly if necessary, to break the habit of obsessive thinking.

Notice also if there is a positive action you would benefit from, such as telling a trusted friend or family member how you feel and what your needs are. Place your feet fully on the ground and feel your connection to the earth. Acknowledge your bravery in feeling a difficult emotion and anticipate more happiness in your life as a result of releasing it.

> *Journal Exercises*
>
> *Are you an obsessively negative person?*
>
> *Do you get stuck in negative thought patterns?*
>
> *Do you feed your negative thought with more self-destructive and self-critical thoughts?*
>
> *Can you connect a negative obsessive thought with its underlying emotion and physical sensation in your body?*
>
> *Can you think of positive statements you can say to yourself to release a negative feeling and replace it with its positive?*
>
> *Do you self-sabotage yourself and others with your judgements of situations?*

Guilt

Every day in your life has something to teach you. If you make a mistake, understand that it is not the end, only part of the learning process in life.

Guilt is when we allow ourselves to feel bad about an event or a person. We feel regret about a situation to the extent that we have taken on blame for the situation. Intense guilt can stop us functioning normally in life. Holding onto it can lead to much unhappiness and illness. There are two kinds of guilt that can trap and block us emotionally:

- **Appropriate guilt:** We've done something wrong. We take responsibility, apologise, get clarity on why we did it, learn from our mistake and let it go.

- **Inappropriate guilt**: We feel a misplaced, toxic guilt as though we've done something wrong when the true reality is we have judged ourselves too harshly, absorbed others' guilt or taken on guilt that others put on us. It does not belong to us.

Appropriate Guilt

Appropriate guilt is culpability we feel that is equal to what we have done. For example, we've done wrong by someone or acted in a way that goes against our values. However, that does not mean we should carry this guilty feeling with us for the long term. Carrying guilt weighs heavily on our minds and is a drain on us mentally and emotionally. Hiding our guilt can cause us to avoid people and situations, and it can affect our confidence and sense of worthiness. We need to sit with it and address it.

Inappropriate Guilt

We are vulnerable to taking on inappropriate guilt if our parents, teachers, boss, or peers have placed extremely high expectations on us. Too much responsibility at a young age, for example, minding younger siblings, can give us a sense of being responsible for things we should not actually be accountable for. If we have a family member who frequently blames and criticises us, telling us we are no good, too nosy, mean, untrustworthy, selfish, or irresponsible, we can start to believe that we often do wrong. If someone close to us gets angry easily, we may find ourselves needing to please and soothe their moods and think that it is our fault if they lose their temper. If we have a strong talent in an area that triggers another's insecurities, their reactions may cause us to reject our potential and feel unworthy of our gift.

When we take on inappropriate guilt, we often feel confused because the guilt does not belong to us, and part of us knows this. As a result, we feel shame and an anger that is directed both inwards and towards others. We can feel haunted and tortured by our thoughts, feel judged, and judgemental of ourselves and others. This may lead to self-destructive patterns, negative obsessive thinking, overeating and addictions, underachievement, self-criticism, working or helping out to the point of exhaustion, feeling constantly resentful, depression or constantly trying to please others to be accepted by them. We may lose our sense of worthiness in all of this misplaced guilt.

How to Release Guilt from the Body

- Bring up your energy. Bring your attention to the present.

- Scan your body. Where does carrying guilt affect you physically? For example, we often carry guilt in the lungs, heart, stomach, shoulders, or intestine.

- Name who started the feelings of guilt. What words were put on you, by yourself or others? What formed the guilt? Separate the types of guilt that you feel.

- First, look at the inappropriate guilt that you are carrying. Look clearly at the people involved in the situation and visualise giving back their harsh judgement and toxic words. If you tend to take on guilt that is not yours, where do you carry it in the body? Mentally give it back and visualise it going back to whom it really belongs. If you are saying harsh words to yourself, stop and let go of what is not true.

- Now, look at the guilt you carry that is appropriate to what happened. Take ownership of what you have done. Take responsibility for your actions. Look at why you did what you blame yourself for. What happened for you to do it? Get some clarity and speak to yourself with compassion. We all make mistakes and are entitled to learn lessons.

- Take the learning from the situation. What triggered you to behave in this way? What do you need to have a look at in yourself? Is there anger, jealousy, impatience, recklessness, loneliness, grief, or a lack of self-confidence behind what you did? Pause for a moment and name your reason for doing what you did. What do you need to do to sort this issue out? Take the learning that is there for you in this mistake. Make a choice never to repeat it.

- Think about what you can do to make amends for your wrongdoing. Look at the bigger picture. Reason with yourself. Apologise if possible. If your apology is not accepted, know that you have tried to make things right. You can't control the reaction of the other person. If it is not possible to make amends with whoever was involved, would it help to do something good to help someone else as your way of healing and balancing the situation within yourself?

- Once you have worked through understanding and resolving the whole situation sincerely, let any residual guilt go. Talk to yourself in a caring way. Let go of self-destructive judgements such as that you are bad. Let go of feeling sorry for yourself. Instead, bring in a feeling of self-forgiveness. Breathe deeply and let this feeling flow through your whole body.

> **Journal Exercises**
>
> How would you describe guilt?
>
> Where did it start?
>
> Is it guilt someone put upon you or guilt that you put upon yourself?
>
> What learning is there for you in the guilt that will help you in the future?
>
> What do you need to let go of?

The Value of Feelings and Learning to Value Our Feelings: Key Points to Remember

- Feelings are meant to be a continuous flow through us, a communication of information, to be felt fully and then allowed to pass through.

- A build-up of uncomfortable emotions in the body causes us distress.

- We can release and replace difficult feelings one at a time giving us relief and a renewed sense of aliveness.

- Worry can be resolved by working backwards from the current worry unpicking and reframing each worry thought back to and including its thought of origin.

- A negative obsessive thought can be dealt with by uncovering, looking at, and replacing the upsetting emotion behind the thought.

- Guilt can be looked at as appropriate and inappropriate guilt. We can hand back and let go of inappropriate guilt and then work through and resolve the guilt that is appropriate to the situation.

Chapter Two

Sleep

A good sleep re-energises us. It improves our thinking processes, our ability to focus, and our moods. It increases our energy levels, promotes better heart function, and gives the immune system precious time to focus on fighting inflammation and infection. During sleep, the pituitary gland releases hormones for the body to grow tissue and repair itself. The muscles relax, and circulation flows much more freely, allowing recovery and replenishment for all the cells and organs. The brain gets a chance to process the day, store information into long-term memory and clean out both unneeded information and waste products. Sleep has various stages, which the body enters cyclically over the course of the night. It includes times of higher brain activity during Rapid Eye Movement (REM) sleep when we do most of our dreaming and deeper states of sleep during non-REM sleep. During non-REM sleep, the levels of cortisol, our stress hormone, lowers significantly, allowing our nervous system time to relax. Over the course of four or more full cycles of these sleep stages, the whole body gets the chance to rest and emerge rebooted into a new day.

Sometimes a good night's sleep evades us. We may have difficulty getting to sleep, slowing down thoughts, often fixating on one particular stress or worry so that we can't seem to drift off. Maybe we fall asleep with relative ease only to wake up in the middle of the night and be unable to return to slumber. We may fall into a deep, heavy sleep for a good number of hours but still be exhausted upon waking. We may sleep too lightly, waking with the slightest disturbance unable to let our defences down to fall into a proper deep sleep. The balance of REM and Non-REM sleep is out of kilter, and sleep can fail to provide you with the recovery needed by your body and mind.

Causes of sleep difficulties include trauma, anxiety and worry, uncertainty, difficult relationships, stressful school or workplaces, being a new parent, shift work, changes in hormones levels, restless legs, illness, snoring, medication, physical pain, addiction, negativity, grief, and depression. We can cope with a poor night's sleep on occasion, but a consistent lack of sleep has a major effect on us, including moodiness, a weakening of the immune system, poor regulation of emotions, slower reaction times, memory loss, a decrease in job productivity or educational achievement and a reduced ability to focus and process thoughts.

Resolving Sleep Difficulties

- Be kind to yourself. Trust your instincts about when the best time for you to sleep is and about how much sleep you need. Try to create a structure in your day that respects whether you are a morning or night person and when in the day, work, exercise, or a nap best suits you. This can be difficult for various reasons but try to create the best routine for yourself.

- Create a bedtime routine for yourself that includes a quiet or soothing activity before bed, such as bathing or reading a book. What helps you to quieten your mind?

- If you can't sleep, don't stay in bed thinking about how difficult your day is going to be without sleep. Instead, get up and have a glass of water or a cup of tea and stay up a short while, allowing your head to clear and then go back to bed and allow sleep to come.

- If you are worried or stressed at night about a particular situation, talk to yourself in a helpful way, looking clearly at it and all the information around the situation. Tune into your logic, intuition, and self-compassion and make a plan for how you can best manage the issue, including where you can access support. Once you have this structure put in place for yourself, it will be easier to sleep.

- Practice night-time breath work before you go to sleep to help you process your day and relax your body.

- Start a daily meditation practice for 10 or 15 mins per day.

- If you regularly have trouble sleeping, seek advice from your GP.

Nightmares

Nightmares are upsetting dreams that can result in night waking and distress. Sometimes that distress is difficult to resolve and can result in us bringing unsettled feelings and thoughts into our day. Dreams and nightmares are caused by changes such as new experiences, hormonal and chemical changes, growth spurts, overloading of the brain with unprocessed thoughts, new learning and realisation, grief, loss, stress, changes in the subconscious and being flooded by another person's emotions. We are more likely to have nightmares at ages of major shifts in our perceptions of the world around us, at age 3, 7, 12/13, 17, and other significant times in our lives.

Changes bring new thoughts and information into our bodies. We often don't manage to keep up with processing how we feel about each one and how each one affects our lives. This causes the pressure of a build-up of emotion and confusion in our bodies. The function of dreams and nightmares is to release this pressure. This is a healthy function of the brain and body. A nightmare runs through the brain, made of a distortion of memories and images in order to release the flood of unprocessed emotions. A rush of adrenaline runs through the body along with overwhelming feelings, and we may wake up with a jump, often sweaty and disoriented.

The key to resolving a nightmare is to look with clarity at the reality of it. The strange scenario that you dreamt of is not real, and therefore there is no value in analysing it or replaying it in your mind. Accept that you had a bad dream and it's ok and reassure yourself that you are ok. The dream itself was just a symbol. You will be able to let that go once you release what was real. The reality of the dream is the feeling that was released. Sit up and put on a light and breathe.

Breathe into the physical discomfort to relax your racing heart and soothe where it affects you in your body. Sit with the feeling of the rush of emotions. Is it worry, anxiety, fear, anger, guilt, or something else? Ask yourself what was it that caused you to feel this way. Name the feeling. Think back through your previous day. For example, if the feeling is worry, were you thinking about exams, your workload or family pressures that caused prickly and uncomfortable feelings? If the feeling was fear, did you see something upsetting on the news which made you fearful or have a near accident that made your mind think about what could have happened? Did you feel very resentful towards someone if the feeling was anger, or did you witness a row? What is going on at the moment in your family life or your school or work setting? Sometimes you may find it difficult to voice how a situation is affecting you.

> *Sometimes we can have enjoyable dreams, ones that give us ideas and inspiration that help us towards our goals. Sometimes we may have dreams about loved ones who have passed, which can help us feel supported and give us guidance and reassurance.*

A nightmare may help you to acknowledge and express the emotion you need to communicate. Question yourself to help you understand where the feeling came from. Accept the feeling. Speak kindly to yourself. Breathe into it. Allow it to be. Say reassuring things to yourself. What support do you need? What positive feeling can you bring in to soothe yourself? What can you say to yourself to give you some support? Do you need to talk to someone? What do you need to say to help you resolve the feeling?

You may still feel a little uncomfortable as your body recovers from the rush of adrenaline that has run through it. If you do not feel ready to go back to sleep, having a drink of water, reading, breathwork, meditating, or getting up and moving around may help you settle, relax, and then get back to sleep.

You will have fewer nightmares if you:

- Process your day before you go to sleep.

- Create structure around things that put pressure on you. For example, make out a realistic study plan coming up to exams. If you are responsible for helping to look after someone, plan exactly what you are prepared to do and where in your week you will do it.

- Make sure you have daily time to relax and do things that you enjoy allowing your mind and body to settle and relax.

- Avoid scary and excessively violent films and computer games, especially just before sleep.

- Eat as healthily as you can and take frequent exercise.

- Talk to someone supportive when you feel upset.

Night-Time Breathwork

This breathwork will help you declutter your thoughts and feel relaxed and ready for sleep in the evening.

- Breathe in and out gently. Calm your heart rate.

- Filter through your thoughts from the day. File away information you have learned. Be aware of negative thoughts. Then, separate your thoughts from other people's negativity, breathe, and mentally give them back their drama and critical thoughts.

- Breathe deeply and release your own negativity.

- Focus on the positives of your day and amplify the good feeling these positives give you.

- Relax your shoulders. Place your hand on your heart, breathing in compassion and the permission to slow down and relax. Relax your lungs and chest. Quieten your stomach. Relax your muscles and bones.

- Imagine your circulation is flowing freely through your whole body.

- Breathe peace, love, light, and healing into your body.

- Feel your body and mind becoming relaxed, calm, and settled, ready for a restful sleep.

> ### *Journal Exercises*
>
> *What disturbs your sleep?*
>
> *What helps you to quieten your mind before sleep?*
>
> *How would you describe the quality of your sleep?*
>
> *How many hours of sleep and what kind of sleep pattern suits you?*
>
> *If you have had a recent nightmare, what emotion was it that came up to be cleared?*
>
> *If you have recurring nightmares, have a look at any anxiety that you hold in your body on an ongoing basis. What can you do to resolve this anxiety?*

> **Sleep: Key Points to Remember**
>
> - Sleep's restorative benefits are essential for our immune system, brain function, nervous system, mood regulation, physical recovery, and energy levels. Therefore, it is important to put a structure in place in our day and night to prioritise a quality night's sleep.
>
> - The upset caused by nightmares can be resolved by addressing the feeling heightened by it rather than by analysing the nightmare itself.
>
> - A practice such as night-time breathwork can help your body prepare for a good night's sleep.

Chapter Three
Arising Panic

We all experience panic at some point in our life. A panicked feeling can be very intense. Panic attacks are related to underlying issues. A present situation may trigger anxiety and fears from the past, of old patterns of thoughts. Our reaction to our current circumstances may cause us to project fear onto our future. An accumulation of emotions causes panic attacks. There is a build-up of worry, and then one small thing can trigger all of the feelings to the surface, and they rush through the body. The areas of the brain which manage our survival instincts, such as the amygdala, become highly activated, flooding the body with hormones whose purpose are to prepare the body to flee, fight, or freeze. Panic attacks are experienced differently by individual people with various levels of outward distress. Hormone imbalances can exacerbate them, and it can be helpful to have tests done through your GP to determine if this is the case for you if you get frequent attacks.

Understanding the Path of Panic Attacks

Panic attacks usually start with the turmoil of racing thoughts. It can feel as if you are attacking yourself with your thoughts. You become extremely negative. A flood of adrenaline is released into your body.

You may feel a constricting, tightening feeling in the top or back of your head. A rush of negative thoughts causes the heart to race and causes tightness in the chest which puts pressure on the lungs. You cannot easily get your breath.

You lack oxygen, resulting in further panic and heightened anxiety and fear, and you feel completely overwhelmed. You may have sweaty hands and feel light-headed. You may feel sick in your stomach. Your stomach muscles may contract, which puts pressure on your intestine and kidneys. The contracted stomach muscle can pulse and feel like you have a beat in your stomach. Other common symptoms include pressure on the collar bone, pins and needles in the hands, restless legs, feeling cold and shivery, dizzy, and dry throat.

If the early signs are not addressed, the panic attack may develop into further contraction of the muscles, fast ineffective breathing, and rapid heart racing. You may feel as if you are suffocating. You feel overwhelmed and out of control. If it gets to this point, it has to run its course. There generally is a peak of 5-10 minutes of complete panic before it begins to dissipate. Create a focus in the present to help you give the panic attack less attention. Ask yourself, "What can I see? What can I hear? What can I touch? What can I smell?" Know that it will peak and pass in a few minutes. Allow people to help and reassure you. It can be frightening, and you need support. Afterwards rest, in a place that feels comforting.

Learning How to Manage the Panic

To stop panic attacks, we have to address the cause. Look at what is the main worry, thought, feeling, or projected worry that is having an impact on your body, triggering the panic. Go into detective mode. Process the information of the worry. Think about the situations that trigger the rush of emotions. Bring the feelings of the situation through your mind. What other times did you feel like that in your life? In your mind's eye, go back to the first time you can remember feeling like that. Tune into the physical sensations in your body. Name the feeling that comes up. Give yourself clarity. What age were you? Visualise yourself having a conversation with the younger anxious you. Talk compassionately to yourself. What support do you need? What kind words can you say to soothe yourself? What specific feeling do you need to give to your younger self? Is it kindness, safety, love, hope, acceptance, confidence? Imagine sending the feeling of this word to where you need it in your body. Feel the difference this makes to you. Feel the power this process gives you.

If you have frequent panic and anxiety attacks, a trusted counsellor could provide the support you need to look at the cause of your panic.

The following example illustrates how one little girl's panic was solved. When she came to see me I observed that this little six-year-old was quite nervous and very clingy to her mum. She had developed an intense fear of dogs for no obvious reason. Whenever she was near a dog, she would cry, become upset, and hyperventilate. She couldn't name the emotion she felt and just thought that dogs made her feel this way. As I worked with her, it came to light that her panic had nothing to do with dogs. Dogs were just a trigger that reminded her of the real cause. One day in the schoolyard, she had experienced being in the presence of two older boys fighting. She had felt enormous fear and had frozen to the spot, internalising her terror. Afterwards, when she saw a dog running towards her, the feelings of witnessing the fight were triggered, causing her to hyperventilate. She started to associate feeling fear with dogs.

Understanding where her panic came from allowed her trapped feelings to be named and released. The next time she saw a dog, she had the clarity to know that it wasn't the dog she feared, and she could breathe into the anxiety and release it. She could breathe the feeling of safety into her body and reassure herself that she was ok.

A Memorable Writing Experience

Since my Mum passed, I have frequently been aware of her presence around me. I felt her presence especially when we were writing about panic. My sense that she was there was validated by a sudden strong smell of cigarette smoke. I felt her opening up an experience for me to see, of what rising panic felt like to her when she was in her thirties and forties and unable to catch her breath. She also shared with me the feeling of her strength and the capacity for love that she developed over the years as she learned to accept her feelings and her life. I treasure this experience for the understanding it gives me of my Mum at various stages of her life and also because it allowed me to feel her continued support of my healing work.

Morning Breathwork

Mornings can often be quite rushed as we strive to get organised and ready on time to start work or school or complete a list of tasks. As a result, our energy and thoughts can become quite scattered, leading to anxiety and stress. We can end up feeling completely frazzled before our day has even properly begun.

The following practice of morning breathwork helps you get ready for your day. It allows your mind and body to come into sync and directs your energy into the day in a more focused way. It helps you to settle into your own time and your own space. When you do this breathwork, you will be surprised by how situations and people cooperate more to help you achieve what you planned for the day. You will get more accomplished with ease.

- Breathe in and out calmly to let go of the adrenaline rush. Become aware of your heartbeat. Think, "I am calming my heart," and breathe in and out slowly to soothe it.

- Feel the connection between your head and your body.

- Imagine a ball of light coming into the bottom of your back. Continue to breathe and allow the light to become stronger and brighter. Allow it to flow up through your back, pulling you together, so you feel present and strong.

- Visualise what you need to do in the day. Imagine your tasks lining up in a manageable way and trust that lots of support is there to help you.

- Be aware of your feet connecting with the ground, anchoring you in your time and space.

- Relax and breathe and be present in yourself as you start your day.

Meditation to Release Anxiety

We all have different anxieties based on our life experience, but now we are going to focus on one anxiety that keeps repeating itself, one that comes in and takes you over, one that holds you back from moving forward, a repeated pattern from the past that keeps coming up for you in the now.

Where are you feeling it in your body? Everyone will feel this differently based on their sensitivity. It can come up in the form of a pain, as pressure on your head or body, as a stuck feeling, a physical sensation, a strong emotion, or an uncomfortable mental thought. You might want to bring up a couple of anxieties, but just come back and sit with one for today.

- Make yourself comfortable either sitting or lying. Close your eyes. Breathe in and out slowly. Become aware of your body from the top of your head, right down to your feet. Ground yourself. Feel strong and present in your body.

- Become aware of your anxiety. Become aware of your breathing. Slow your breathing down. Where do you feel it in your body? What anxious thoughts keep coming up in your present, holding you back, pulling you out of the present, giving you a feeling of being overwhelmed, irritable or unable to cope with people or situations. Think about what you usually do to distract yourself from these thoughts and feelings, such as keeping yourself busy, using your phone, withdrawing from your family or friends, or snacking on food. Have you formed some habits to release anxiety such as nail-biting, fidgeting, blinking, biting your lip, cracking your fingers or neck, or engaging in self-harm? What do you do when you feel anxious?

- Allow your anxiety to heighten so you can name it and resolve it. If you were to name that anxiety, what name would you put on it? Be aware of what is heightening in you physically, emotionally, and mentally. Where in your body feels the pressure of this anxiety? What other emotions are behind this anxiety? What thoughts caused it?

- Be aware of your energy inside you and all around you, above you and below you, in front of you, and behind you. Where is the sensation the strongest?

- Visualise white light down into the top of your head. Let your energy field fill with this white light. Let it flow all around you, above, below, in front, and behind. Now pay attention to where your body holds the anxiety and flood that area with white light. Let the white light move inside you, healing wherever this anxiety has affected you - your organs, circulation, muscles, and bones. You are going to bring in a positive word to heal this anxiety. What is the best word? Change the anxious word into a positive. Let it be love, security, peace, fun, acceptance. Whatever you need. Bring in your strengths, your power of healing, and your identity of self. Feel your connection to this positive word getting stronger.

- Feel what has changed in you, physically, emotionally, and mentally. Welcome peace into your mind, love in your heart, and light and healing in your body.

- Allow the white light to move around the top of your head, illuminating the brain and spinal cord. Allow the light to flow all around the head and into the eyes. Let it move slowly into the face and neck and flow down into the body into the organs, glands, tissues, and bones, the chest, the heart, lungs, the stomach, and the pelvis, nicely and slowly. Let it flow through your body, correcting muscle and circulation. Let it flow down your arms and hands and your legs into your feet and right out the bottom of your feet.

Trust in the exercise you have done and in how you are learning to heal your anxiety. Don't question it. Acknowledge the difference in how you feel physically, emotionally, and mentally. Feel yourself grounded. Slowly open your eyes. Be present. Be here. Be now.

Welcome change, face the anxiety and fear.
Look at the situation with clarity, and you will be surprised at the outcome.
Be positive; all will change for the better.

> **Journal Exercises**
>
> *Do you experience panic attacks?*
>
> *If so, how would you describe the panic attacks?*
>
> *Where in the body do you feel it?*
>
> *What emotions, thoughts, or situations trigger it?*
>
> *Is your panic caused by a fear of not being able to cope with the future?*
>
> *Is your panic caused by you not being able to accept an aspect of yourself?*
>
> *Do you need the support of a counsellor to help identify and work through the cause of your panic?*
>
> *What are your early signs of a panic attack coming on?*
>
> *What works for you to help you calm down when you feel panic?*
>
> *How can you soothe yourself out of a full-scale panic attack?*

Stepping Back - When Panic Attacks Reoccur

By the time I was in my late thirties, I was well used to the overwhelming, overpowering, and paralysing ambush of panic. I had my first attack when I was 14, and as the years went on, they became clusters visiting me depending on the events of my life. Finally, at thirty-nine, as a rising swell began and I felt those first moments of fear and panic travel through my body, I said to myself, "No more. I can't do this anymore. I don't want this." I knew at that moment, as the familiar feeling crept in, that I had to let them go.

With this thought, I committed myself to staying in the present and observing these panic attacks as much as I could. It took time, but over the following months, I felt an inner strength build within me. During my twenties and thirties, an underlying fear beneath my skin where I felt the panic reside, had settled in me as though I could lose my mind in the midst of these attacks, but the difference was I was now summoning the courage to face that fear and everything attached to it.

And so, as those familiar feelings took hold, panic flooded my body once again. I felt a heat in my core, a clammy chill in my limbs, and I started to sweat. My stomach knotted in a pulsing throb as the panic took hold, and my mind surrendered to the trepidation. Images from my past danced in front of me like crumbling shadows as a band tightened around my chest. I was breathing. Fast and shallow.

I tried to focus. I told myself to breathe, that the danger was subconsciously held, that my body was reacting, and that my lungs were working perfectly if I just allowed them to inhale slowly. However, when panic hits, it truly hits like a double-decker bus or the weight of a rhino. I felt as though my lungs would explode under the excruciating pressure building in my chest. Fighting through this intensity is a significant challenge for any of us, whether it's our first or fiftieth attack. This was to be my last, and as I stayed focusing on my breathing, I remained present with that physical, severe pain searing through my breastbone, lifting my chest.

I stayed. I kept breathing. I let go. Suddenly, there was a shift in my awareness, and for a few moments, it felt as though I was almost rising out of my body and looking down on myself. The air shifted around me as if time had been suspended and a floodgate opened. That intense pressure was released, and a freedom and relief flowed into my arms and chest as my breath deepened. I was letting go.

The panic subsided, and an intense feeling of compassion encircled me as I released the emotional burden I had been carrying for so long. Support, unconditional love, and affection surrounded me, along with a knowing that presence can heal my past. And with that, I was ok.

I am ok.

Arising Panic: Key Points to Remember

- Panic attacks are very common and are related to an accumulation of fear, trauma, and unhelpful patterns of thought which have been unresolved and stored in the body. They are like a mental and emotional earthquake in the body.

- Early signs of an oncoming panic attack include racing negative thoughts and a feeling of tightness in the muscles and organs.

- To lessen the impact of a panic attack, consciously deepen and slow your breathing, keep an attitude of self-compassion, and use all of your strength to stay in the present by tuning into your five senses.

- When in the peak of a panic attack, know that it will soon pass and then take gentle care of yourself when it does.

- Get the support you need to find and face the cause of your anxiety by confiding in a trusted friend, making an appointment with a Cognitive Behaviour Therapist who can help you change distorted thinking and beliefs and help you learn new ways to cope, asking your GP to refer you to Primary Care Psychology, or by ringing the *Samaritans* which offer free support to anyone in emotional distress.

- Get out ahead of anxiety in your day by doing the morning breathwork exercise or the meditation to release anxiety.

Chapter Four

Connection and Disconnection

At any moment in time, you are either connected to or disconnected from yourself.

When we feel fully connected, we feel plugged into our own power, a strong bond with and compassion for other people, connected to a caring higher consciousness and an appreciation for the beauty of the planet that supports our lives. When we are connected, we are present in the here and now, in the moment, physically, emotionally, mentally, and spiritually. We are tuned into our bodies, aware of our emotions, thoughts, and gut instincts and how these affect us. We know which thoughts and emotions are not ours, such as others' strong opinions or anger, and we can let these go. Connection brings a feeling of self-acceptance. We appreciate our own gifts and nurture them, and do not compare ourselves to others. We follow our own path, knowing who we are, working to be the best we can be. Connection brings contentment. We take ownership of our beliefs, values, and morals and speak our truth. We feel hopeful about the future.

A feeling of connection with other people allows us to relax in our relationships and enjoy them. We see people as having a shared human experience just with different personalities and life experiences which cause them to think and act in various ways. We have more compassion and understanding in our interactions with each other. We feel like we belong even if things aren't currently working out as we might have hoped.

Connection to a higher consciousness, God, the source, or the Divine gives us access to unconditional support in our lives, depending on our faith. Connection with nature allows us to feel the sustenance that the earth provides for us and to appreciate the beauty of the natural world around us.

When we are connected, there is a rich flow of energy flowing through us, out from us to other people, the Divine, and nature, and we are open to lots of energy flowing back to us. We are seen, heard, supported, and very alive.

Disconnection

To disconnect is to let go of being present. When we are disconnected from ourselves, we can't hear what people are saying to us. We easily lose our flow of thought in a conversation. We may arrive at a destination without noticing the journey or sit in class or our workplace and be totally unaware of what is happening around us. The thoughts we are thinking belong to either the past or the future. They may even be someone else's thoughts and opinions. Allowing most of our thinking to wander from the present can give rise to over-analysing and worry, resulting in distorted thoughts. We unconsciously make up stories about other people and their actions.

We may be forgetful, frequently drop things, or be prone to accidents. When disconnected, it is exceedingly difficult to focus and make decisions because we are not in tune with our feelings, logical thought, or gut instincts. Being disconnected can give us a sense of being out of our body or out of control and of not being noticed or valued. We get flooded with thoughts and emotions, a mixture of our own things that we had suppressed and thoughts and feelings from people around us that resonates with our present state. We feel negative, anxious, insecure, and angry because we are cut off from our personal power. We feel like we don't belong. We may find ourselves creating personalities to fit in or to try to cope, but in doing so lose our true identity and end up feeling isolated and lonely and not liking ourselves very much.

Our disconnection is at the root of our arguments, poor judgement, negativity, depression, anger, and lack of care. It creates an attitude of *them and us* or more concerning *them and me* which can lead to many wide-ranging troubles such as crime, delinquency, serious addiction, or suicidal thoughts.

Causes of Disconnection

We are born with a craving for connection with our parents and the world around us. If our need is not met in early childhood, it can result in us closing in on ourselves and shutting down our connection with others for fear of future hurt or disappointment.

We disconnect when we lose our trust in the present moment. A current situation triggers a strong unwanted emotion, and so we allow our presence to leave. We disconnect when we worry about the future. Our thoughts go into imagined scenarios, planning on how to cope with or avoid situations.

Also, replaying the past because we have held onto guilt, judgement, or regret causes disconnection. Experiencing a sudden shock or trauma, feeling overwhelmed, thinking negatively, being fearful, or losing a loved one can all cause us to disconnect.

How to Reconnect

Connection is our natural state. When we take away the reason for our disconnection and decide to reconnect, we are automatically back in our power. If we have experienced early deprivation of a loving adult connection, we have to understand and acknowledge what we have missed out on. Likewise, if we have gone through trauma, we would benefit from going back and doing some healing work on ourselves. A supportive therapist could help us find what we have to do to lessen the effects of that experience, help us think in a different way and open up to a greater sense of connection again in our lives.

The following guidance and meditation will help you spend more of your time in a state of connection.

- Regularly check in with yourself to see if you are present in your body. Notice when you are doing things to get to the next moment and are feeling constantly frustrated. Notice if your thoughts are in the past or future instead of the present. Ask yourself, "Where am I gone? What's wrong? Am I immersed in my past? What triggers take me back into my past? Am I regularly consumed with fearful thoughts about the future, the 'what ifs?' and self-doubting thoughts? Do I need to work on my self-belief and my self-worth?"

- Decide to be brave enough to stay in the present moment. What emotions are you suppressing in your body? What have you taken on from other people? Who do you carry pain for? Where do you feel pain or discomfort in your body? Bring the information through your body. What do you need to acknowledge? What thoughts and emotions are coming up to be released? What thoughts, opinions, or feelings are affecting you that belong to others? Mentally give them back their information, clearing it from your body and mind.

- Choose to be present and to come back into your body. Call your full presence back. The benefits of connection will allow you to have clarity and give you access to your power. Your strength and true self is in the present moment.

- Use your breath to reconnect. Take a few long, slow deep breaths, pausing after each in-breath.

- Use your sensory perceptions. Ask yourself what you can hear, smell, touch, taste, and see.

- Imagine standing in a huge tube of light energy which protects you in the here and now.

- Welcome yourself back into your present.

Make sure to give some time to activities each day that allow you to feel present easily. It may be chatting to a group of friends about an interest such as soccer and getting to share your knowledge and opinions. It may be chatting about an issue and how you and others feel about it. It may be working on a project or listening to music, whatever gives you a feeling of flowing along in the present moment.

When we are reconnected, we listen and stop before reacting. We hear what others have to say. We are true to ourselves in our responses and actions. We feel positive in ourselves and know that we have support and can cope with our day.

Being in the Here and Now Meditation

This is a lovely meditation to bring you into the present, be in the here and now and feel comfortable with self.

- Bring up your energy.

- Be aware of your breathing. Allow your breathing to become relaxed within the rhythm of your heart.

- Be present in the here and now, in your time and space, allowing your energy to flow through your body from the top of your head to the bottom of your feet and all around your body, clearing your energy field.

- Allow the energy to continue to flow out through the bottom of your feet, grounding you, rooting you to the ground.

- Be aware of your backbone. Visualise it in 3D, seeing the discs of your spine, the bone marrow, the nerve endings, and the surrounding muscle. Bring in white light to bring strength into this area.

- Become aware of the tension in the muscle in your body. Let it go. Relax.

- Be mindful of your thoughts. Allow them to flow in and out. Quieten the mind, without judgement, in a caring way with self.

- Become aware of your thoughts and allow them to flow in and out through your mind. Having an awareness of this happening allows your mind to become still. Be free. Be quiet. Be still. We question the stillness and quietness as we are not used to this. If your mind does this, allow it through and quieten the mind again in a calm and caring way without thought.

- Visualise six pillars of white light, one in front of you, each side of you and behind you, above you and below you. Allow it to connect as a whole circle around you, protecting you, healing you and grounding you.

- Become aware of your breath and your presence in the here and now. You may feel pressure in the body. Allow it to clear without judgement or thought. Feel how powerful and strong your energy and vibration has become.

- Become aware of the heart, allowing the heart to relax.
- Quieten the mind, clear the mind.
- Imagine purple light coming into your frontal brain, allowing your brain activity to slow and become calm.
- Allow the purple light to flow through your whole head and face allowing your hearing to heighten and your sense of smell to be clear.
- Become aware of the thought, allowing blue light to fill your mind. Listen to your inner voice, the voice of truth, the voice of self. Information will now flow more freely from within, giving you clarity.
- Allow your heart to open, flooding it with pink light.
- Relax the lungs. Relax the chest.
- Visualise white light coming into the breastbone, the stomach and the backbone and spreading out, touching every fibre, organ, and cell in your body through peace, love, light, and healing.
- Focus on white light flowing into the area three inches down from your belly button, into your intuition. Feel connected. Feel a heightened sense of oneness with self.
- Acknowledge the feeling of being present in the here and now and feeling comfortable with self.
- Acknowledge your heightened sense of purpose and inspiration.
- Feel your connection, through your feet, with the earth, grounding you.

> **Journal Exercises**
>
> *How often do you disconnect?*
>
> *Where do you drift off to when you disconnect?*
>
> *What do you not want to see, hear, or feel when you disconnect?*
>
> *What are you losing out on in your life when you are not present?*
>
> *How do you reconnect?*

Stepping Back - Learning to Reconnect

About ten years ago, a client arrived and sat in front of me with a stern face and folded arms, clearly very uncomfortable to be in the position where someone was looking at him expecting him to say something about himself. We had a mutual friend, and this gave me some opening chat. He slowly turned the conversation to his marriage and how he thought it was over. He felt very angry because he had worked so hard for years providing for his wife and children, late nights and weekends. He had also recently lost his dad to cancer. He snapped that he didn't really know why he came, and I knew I had a couple of minutes to help him before he bolted.

I had been reading his energy from the moment he had walked in. Images of him from childhood popping into my mind, emotions he had locked away lighting up in his energy field, guidance from his dad in the spirit world coming into my right ear. I took a deep breath and let all the information flow. I described in some detail traumatic things he had experienced as a child and identified the ages he had been for each one. I had his full attention now, bewilderment showing on his face. These were life events that he had never told anyone about. Finally, he started to open up, confirming what I was saying, arms unfolding as we talked. He laid out the difficulties that existed in his family and how that now manifested in strained relationships between his siblings in present times.

I pointed out that his lower back pain and stomach issues were caused by his inability to cope with how he felt as a child, which led to him shutting down, thus reducing his ability to feel. I acknowledged that he had worked very hard to provide for his family but that he had never properly shown up emotionally in his relationship and that his wife felt very lonely and unseen by him. However, I told him that it wasn't too late for him to turn things around and that he just needed to explain to her why he had been so distant and make a sincere effort to show her that he valued her as his partner in life, that he appreciated all she had done in rearing their two children and was prepared to open up emotionally to her as he worked on healing his trauma.

During the following year, he came to see me three more times. I admired him for the ways in which he reconnected with himself, his wife, and his teenagers over the course of this time.

Loneliness

Be visible to you, and everyone will see you.
Shine within yourself. Be your own person.

Loneliness is a feeling of being detached and isolated from self and others. It is a feeling of not belonging, of not being seen or of not being understood. It is a particular kind of sadness and something we all feel at various times in our lives.

Loneliness can bring in other emotions, too, such as fearfulness and anxiety. When you feel lonely, it is more difficult to cope with everyday challenges. You may feel jealous of other people who seem to belong and appear happy. You may feel a physical ache in your heart, back, head, or stomach. You may get a bit stuck in your head thinking negative thoughts and feeling sorry for yourself. Over analysing can lead to distorted or paranoid thinking.

Intense loneliness can cause excess adrenaline in our bodies which leads to exhaustion. People may create addictions, such as food, medications, or online gaming, to try and avoid feeling their loneliness. Hidden loneliness can bring in feelings of despair because we may portray outwardly that we are okay, and others don't see our pain. For example, suppose we don't communicate how we feel to trusted family and friends and work towards resolving our loneliness. In that case, we can feel depressed, like we have fallen into a bleak part of ourselves, unable to climb out. We may end up fearing our thoughts, being terrified of them being suicidal.

The Internal Causes of Loneliness

Loneliness has many causes. What they have in common is that something happened to shock you, which triggered emotions that made you question your place in the world. It may have been caused by one or more of these factors:

- Your mother's high anxiety level while you were in the womb.
- Your birth being traumatic for you and your parents.
- Being abandoned or feeling rejected by your parents.
- A frequent lack of needed reassurance.
- Not being seen or listened to during childhood.
- Important information not being shared or explained to you, such as a parent's illness.
- Being bullied.
- Being a new parent.
- Being highly sensitive and feeling different.

- Having depression.
- Suffering from anxiety. This can cause you to create a small world for yourself to help you feel secure.
- Finding it hard to cope with the different stages of development and growth, such as childhood into the teenage years and retirement.
- Transitions such as moving to a new house, changing schools, or starting college.
- Separation and family break up.
- A parent going to prison.
- Grief. The death of a loved one.
- Hardships, such as a job loss.
- Difficulty making friends.
- Poverty or debt.
- Having a disability.
- Rebelling as a teenager.
- Having an ongoing illness.
- Having a family member who needs a lot of care and attention.
- Choosing a group of friends that don't reflect who you really are and then trying to fit in.
- Boredom.
- Having fertility complications.

- Being confused about or not accepting your sexuality.
- Carrying loneliness for a family member or friend.
- Traumatic experiences.
- A controlling parent, partner, or friend.
- Guilt.

How to Manage Loneliness

Unresolved feelings of loneliness can be triggered by different experiences throughout our lives.

- Sit and reflect. Go back and find where the loneliness started for you. It was possibly in childhood. Acknowledge the first significant event in your life that made you feel lonely. Resolve the lonely feelings you have held in your body for years. Then work on more recent situations that have triggered your loneliness in a similar way. Once you have resolved these situations, you will only ever have to deal with the loneliness that arises in the present.

- Allow yourself to accept who you are (your body, family origins, colour, abilities, sexuality, sensitivity, and past traumas) and then open up to allow the positive people in your life to support you.

- Create a list of people who are your support team, such as a parent, friend, teacher, co-worker, and siblings. Focus on the emotional support you get from them rather than the parts of your life where you feel unsupported.

- Know there is huge power in saying how you really feel to people you trust.

- Make a conscious decision to be hopeful.
- Resolve to find your place in society.
- Reclaim your place in the world. Visualise bringing your place in the world under your feet. Feel grounded. Accept yourself, take back your control, trust, belief, and faith. Acknowledge your strength. Dream big and believe in yourself.
- Live day by day, find your own identity and live being true to your real self.
- Change your environment. Leave your bedroom or get off the couch and call to see people you love and who you know will support you, reaching out for their kindness and understanding.
- Encourage yourself to get involved in the community; be active and socialise. By helping and supporting other people, you will feel connected with others. A class or club that interests you is a great way to find your tribe of like-minded people.

If you are feeling very intense loneliness and do not have friends or family to turn to, there are many organisations at hand to help, such as *Jigsaw* for teenagers and young adults, *Alone* for older people and the *Samaritans*.

Journal Exercises

At what times have you experienced loneliness in your life?

Do you sometimes feel lonely because you have disconnected from yourself?

Which personal strengths, qualities, or activities do you need to focus on to help you reconnect with yourself?

Do you sometimes feel lonely due to a lack of connection with a friend group?

Do you isolate yourself? If so, why do you choose to be alone?

What are your interests or hobbies that you can use to join a class or club?

Connection and Disconnection: Key Points to Remember

- Connection arises when the flow of life energy is open through our whole body and we are open to linking with the flow of energy of other people, Divine energy, and the natural world. It is the choice to live in relationship with ourselves, others, the earth, and the Source.

- We disconnect to avoid pain but in staying disconnected we create more.

- When we bring awareness and compassion to why we have disconnected we can open up again to connection.

- Loneliness can be resolved by addressing the original event that made us feel lonely and then being open to finding connection with ourselves, supportive people and our community.

Chapter Five

Negativity

Negativity starts with a thought that repeats itself, such as, "Today is going to be a hard day." If you don't challenge the thought and change it to a more positive one, more negative thoughts join it, which brings in a low feeling. This feeling distorts the thought, and you can become more self-destructive in your thinking, accumulating more uncomfortable thoughts.

For example, if you have an important exam and you start thinking, "What if I can't remember what I've learned?" you then start imagining all the consequences of doing badly. This brings in corresponding feelings of worry, anxiety, panic, and guilt. Then you start remembering when you felt like this before and the circumstances at those times, and you use evidence from those situations to make negative statements about yourself and others. Next, you start believing that the rabbit hole of distorted thinking you have just fallen into is producing profound truths and realisations instead of seeing it as the poisonous concoction you have created because you didn't challenge that first negative thought. Your blood temperature rises. Your skin feels irritated. Blood flow is restricted, and your muscles tighten. You feel pain in your body and pity for yourself, which can heighten your negativity even more.

Spend a moment to look back at your life in the negatives and the positives. Let go of the negativity and acknowledge everything positive in your life. Set your purpose and goals with clarity in a positive way.

The following feelings, attitudes and situations feed and amplify our negativity:

- Suppressed anger.
- Resentment of a situation and believing things are not fair.
- Guilt
- Listening to other people's negativity and getting into the habit of thinking about things the way they do.
- Being impatient and expecting everyone around you to see and meet your needs first.
- Having a lack of self-confidence, low self-belief, and feeling insecure.
- Past regrets.
- Being jealous or envious of other people or situations.
- Having a lack of respect for yourself or others.
- Worrying excessively about future events.
- Living your life in a way expected by others that is contrary to your true self.
- Having a negative family member due to their life experiences or experiences going back through the generations.
- Being stressed about work or financial pressures.

- Having friends who are negative, who constantly moan about people and situations. Negativity is contagious!

Resolving Negativity

We can all get into a habit of negativity, making ourselves and others unhappy. Becoming aware of your thoughts gives you the power to break the habit. As you listen to your thoughts, notice how negative thoughts impact you and others. Trace your negativity back to its source. You might need to say what was originally bothering you out loud to someone who listens well but resist the temptation to add to it, dramatise it, or encourage them to feed your negativity with theirs. You needn't stay in it. Don't let it take you over. You can take the power out of the negativity by addressing what is really going on with you. Then deal with it. Decide to let it go.

Follow this guidance to help you. Sit with it. Feel it. Name it. Let it go and bring in the positive.

- Is it yours, or does it belong to another? Trace your current flow of negativity back to where it started. Is your negativity the result of someone else's anger, worry, fear, or resentment? If it wasn't yours to start with, mentally hand it back to the owner and clear it from your mind.

- If it was yours, what caused it? Bring the original negative thought through your mind, name the thought and feeling that started the negativity and let them go. Take it out of your head and drop it into an imaginary bin. Choose a more positive thought to replace it with. Let go of the feeling that the thought created and replace it with its opposite. Thinking about your values, potential, dreams for your future, and the sort of person you want to be will help inspire some excellent replacement thoughts.

- You have a choice to be positive or negative, to hold onto old negative patterns of thinking or to teach your flow of thought a new route bringing negative thoughts one by one through your mind and transforming them.

Learning to do this does take time. The key is to catch yourself early. It is easy to change one thought rather than wait to act when many other thoughts have joined. You can develop your own style of coping with your day in a constructive way as you practice focusing on thoughts that soothe you and help you be positive. The rewards are amazing! Practising resolving your negativity brings positivity, happiness, achievement of potential and a profound feeling of being the creator of your own life. This is because old patterns of thought and the negativity of others lose their control over you. You become your own complete person.

Stop saying, "I wish. If only. I don't care. Life is hard."

Start saying, "I will. I want. I am. I love."

> ### *Journal Exercises*
>
> *Do you describe yourself as a negative or positive person?*
>
> *Do you speak negatively in your head?*
>
> *Where in your body do you feel negative?*
>
> *What or who causes you to be negative? What are your triggers?*
>
> *If you are frequently negative is it due to: difficult life experiences, learned behaviour from your parents, or is it an attitude you have adopted to give yourself a sense of authority?*
>
> *What sort of things do you say to yourself in the morning as you start your day?*
>
> *What do you need to do to change your negativity into positivity?*

Feeling A Bit Stuck

Sometimes in life, we fall into a pattern of habits, giving us the feeling of being stuck.

Change and release the habit. This will allow you to move forward.

Everyone feels a bit stuck in their life at some stage. Are you feeling stagnant in your life at present? Does the following describe you? You gather thoughts and feelings and don't let go of them. You allow these thoughts to ruminate around and around in your mind and body, clumping together and getting distorted. You are like a pond of stagnant water where nothing flows through. You lack energy and enthusiasm. You feel a bit lost in yourself and that life is happening around you. You have difficulty motivating yourself to fulfil the demands of a job, study, or do household tasks. You can be cranky and defensive, feeling you are not listened to or understood and that things are generally unfair in your life. You believe your effort makes little difference, so why bother. You enjoy the sympathy you get from others when you complain about the way things never work out for you. You lose a lot of time on mindless activities such as watching TV, gaming, being on your phone, sleeping in, or excessive snacking. You gather others around you who feel similarly so you can all hide together instead of addressing your issues and stepping out into life as your true selves.

Overcoming That Stagnant Feeling

When this type of energy permeates our lives, we need to create some momentum. Here are four steps to get us started:

1. **Decide to stop blaming yourself and others** for how you feel. Decide to love yourself. Commit to taking back your control, trust, belief, and faith in yourself. Take ownership of yourself. If you have thoughts and feelings you have trouble with, commit to seeking help with these. With support from a friend, parent, teacher, or counsellor, you'll be able to see what's real and what's not real. Distorted thoughts can be held up to the light and released.
2. **Help someone else.** Look around you. Who could do with your helping hand and kind heart? Visit a lonely neighbour, do some chores for a family member, cook someone a surprise dinner, help with a DIY project, or helpfully share your talents in your community. This will help you look out at the world instead of always looking in and give you a greater connection with others and a sense of your power to do good.
3. **Try something new.** Think of the things you were passionate about when you were younger. Was it art, being out in nature, baking, music, writing, athletics, horse riding, making things,

being with animals, or something else? Be inspired. Take a class or join a club. This will get your creativity and life-force flowing and give you glimpses of your potential.
4. **Change your environment.** Move the furniture in your bedroom or paint it with a fresh new colour. Declutter your space. Go outside for at least 20 minutes a day. If things have gotten very toxic for you in your work environment, consider changing your place of work to give yourself a new start. Even small changes in your environment can kick start your journey out of a rut.

As you start to feel the buzz of momentum in your life, seek help from a supportive person to help you work through any self-sabotaging thoughts that need resolving. Practise speaking kindly to yourself with compassion and optimism. Change your habits of thought from overthinking the problems in your life to focusing on possible solutions. Make goals for yourself and start taking small steps towards them. Get into the habit of decision making, small decisions first, such as planning a weekend away. Next, look at medium ones, such as decisions around work, college courses, and lifestyle. Decide what your values, strengths, and interests are and then you'll be ready for the bigger decisions, such as your career long-term, where you'd like to live, and decisions around relationships. Make a daily routine for yourself so that your day reflects your decisions and choices, and you are living with purpose, moving in the direction of your goals. Remember to spend time on the things you love to do. Make having fun a priority in your life!

As you move forward in your life, focus less on trying to control the way others see you and instead seek your security from your connection to your true self.

Journal Exercises

Do you complain about things being unfair?

Do you feel unfulfilled?

What do you opt out of?

Do you fear being rejected? If so, what do you fear being rejected for?

Make a list of things that you enjoy doing.

Focus on your life purpose and goals.

Create some goals for yourself

Short Term Goals

_____

_____

Medium Term Goals

_____

_____

Long Term Goals

_____

_____

Stepping Back - Washing Away Negativity

As a mother in my late twenties, raising my three sons to be the best of who they are, was my main focus. Naturally, I worried about their safety and health. And just like any mother whose marriage was becoming more and more difficult, my thoughts were sometimes obsessive. There was an underlying feeling of being controlled in my life, and because of that, there were days when I found I simply couldn't focus and struggled to think clearly. During that time, which was a very difficult period in my life, I was flooded by waves of negative thinking. I suffered long periods of depression and had suicidal thoughts.

Along with the deterioration of my mental well-being, I had further health issues and chronic pain. Solpadine was all I knew to relieve the pain, and addiction ensued. I felt like I was losing the sense of who I was. It was only when I started counselling, meditation and working on myself that I began to regain a sense of my identity. I began to look at my difficult life experiences instead of trying to hold it all in. Gradually my thinking changed, and as my negativity became watered down, I could wean myself off the medication and take back responsibility for myself and my own power.

I still had times of feeling irritable and overwhelmed, but I had started to find my coping skills. I was learning to find my own thoughts and to check in with my feelings. I could take myself out of these dips in my mood by consciously and repeatedly deciding to stop looking back and instead focus on my road ahead. I had found myself again. I could deal with my emotions each day. My gifts and abilities started to open up in a whole new way. I could trust that everything was going to be okay. My inner spirit was bringing me into the light of myself. I could do this on my own.

Hormones

Hormones are essential chemical substances that act like messenger molecules in the body. After being produced in one part of the body, they travel to other parts to help control how cells and organs do their work. Hormones regulate physiological activities in the body, such as melatonin which promotes sleep, ghrelin and leptin which regulate appetite, serotonin which stabilises mood, oestrogen, progesterone, and testosterone which control reproduction and insulin which helps control our blood sugar levels.

Changing hormone levels affect us physically but can also impact us emotionally and mentally, making us more prone to negativity and feelings of being overwhelmed. These hormone shifts can be extremely hard to cope with. We can find that our emotional reaction to situations radically changes over a number of weeks or months.

Between the ages of 10 to 16, there is a surge of hormones in the brain that help reorganise our brain function, transitioning the brain from a child's brain to that of an adult's and the body from a child's body to an adult's. For some people, this surge can happen very suddenly, and for others, it can happen more gradually. The hormone surge changes the range of feelings and the intensity of emotions we feel. We can feel moody, angry, sad, lonely, and confused. The volume of information we take in greatly increases as our brain's ability to perceive, and process develops.

We also experience shifts in hormone levels at other life stages. For women, this occurs during pregnancy, after childbirth, and during menopause. For men, it occurs in their mid-forties to early fifties. They may find themselves doing a mid-life review that can turn into a mid-life crisis. They evaluate their lives, including their work, relationship, and lifestyle. It's common in this state to ask questions such as:

"Is there more for me?"

"What's missing in my life?"

Divine Energy Insight, Healing and Potential

"Can I really face staying in this job or career?"

"Why am I not happy in my relationship?"

This can happen for women, too but usually not as suddenly. If we have a rush of such thoughts, we can tend to make sudden changes in our lives. However, these actions may not fill our void. It can lead to a happier life in the long-term if we take a step back and get clarity about what we need to put into our lives, to put things right for us, following a considered plan to achieve our goals, in a way that is fair to our loved ones and gentler for ourselves.

When we don't cope well with hormonal changes, it can lead to:

- Sudden outbursts of anger.
- Frequent crying.
- Forgetfulness.
- Loss of confidence.
- Being argumentative.
- Off-loading our emotions onto other people.
- Blaming other people for things that aren't their fault.
- Physical aggression.
- Low moods and depression.
- Negative thinking.
- Verbal aggression.
- Obsessive, compulsive behaviour.
- Being reckless.
- Rebellion against authority or responsibility.

When you notice an overreaction to a situation or a random unexplained intensity of emotion, it may be due to a significant change in your hormone levels. When this happens, you need to create some space for yourself. Practise *The Calm Breath*. You will know and value a feeling of your own space and create it very quickly with repeated practice. After doing this exercise, you will find that there is now a space to contain the feeling. In this way, you can gain control of yourself and your reaction. You can acknowledge that your level of emotion is larger than the situation and take responsibility for your subsequent actions and words instead of finding fault with loved ones as an excuse for your feelings and behaviour. For example, if you frequently feel incredibly angry, you needn't clash with people. Instead, create your space. React calmly to whoever is around you and then find an appropriate way to release your anger, such as punching a punch bag, lifting weights, or going for a run, walking, or swimming. Attending counselling may help you navigate this new stage in your life. In mid-life, asking your GP to check your hormone levels and taking prescribed replacement hormones if needed can help to bring back your equilibrium.

As you go through hormone shifts, you can balance spending time with others and doing something you enjoy on your own. Having your own space and time to read, draw, write, listen to music, fish, design things, or exercise really helps you settle into the newer version of you that your hormones are helping to create.

> *Journal Exercises*
>
> *Have you recently experienced sudden hormone-induced changes in mood or rushes of emotions?*
>
> *Where in your body does a change in hormone levels impact?*
>
> *What do you need to do to nurture and support yourself during this time?*

Stepping Back - Teenage Angst

My early teens, was a particularly hard time for me as it often is for many kids. For me, those teenage years were fraught with a troubled home life, the inability to understand my heightened sensitivity, combined with all of those teenage hormones rushing invariably throughout my growing body and mind. I was the very epitome of a pendulum, swinging back and forth with a fierce inability to slow down and rationalise my thoughts, process my feelings, and calm my mind. It goes without saying that I had a distinctly poor sense of who I was and where I fitted in.

We often think no one is watching, no one understands, or no one wants to listen. But look around. There's often someone there. My Aunt Maura saw me struggling. The type of woman to recognise an inner turmoil before someone realised it themselves, she took me under her wing. I would help her with housework, and as we dusted and preened, we'd chat, having compassionate conversations which not only made time disappear but gave me a different viewpoint on life, the world, and my very being. Through these engaging heart-to-hearts, she encouraged me to see life more optimistically. Her wisdom and kindness emboldened me to believe more in myself and value myself in a way I may not have were it not for her gentle guidance. Aunt Maura often brought me along to prayer meetings where the atmosphere of prayer, meditation, and song stirred a strong connection to the spiritual side of myself. Through Aunt Maura and the path she brought me along, I found I could appease and let go of anger and upset, relax, and settle into my own time and space.

Negativity: Key Points to Remember

- Negativity starts with a thought. Left unchecked more negative thoughts follow that one. Getting out of negativity is about catching this flow of thought early and turning it around.

- Resolve negativity by taking the time to sit with it, feel it, name its cause, let it go, and then bring in some positive thoughts and feelings.

- By identifying what amplifies our negativity we can work on changing attitudes and circumstances over a period of time to allow more happiness into our lives.

- If you feel a bit stuck or stagnant in your life, the keys to moving forward are to let go of blame, try new things, help other people, and change your environment for the better.

- When hormonal shifts cause or add to our negativity we can create our own space and time, to give ourselves the chance to process these changes and adjust.

Chapter Six

Pain

Pain can start with negative thoughts, which we repeat over and over and analyse at a negative level. Over time this causes muscles to contract in our bodies. Circulation is not allowed to flow freely through an area of the body, and we feel pain. Therefore pain is a call for us to pay attention to our negativity and to release it, which allows circulation to flow freely and for us to feel better.

Pain can also show us from where emotions, shock, and trauma need to be released in the body. The body is saying, "Look here; Open here; Feel here; Bring love and care here!" The combination of medical assistance where needed and the release of stored emotions and thoughts is an effective way to manage ongoing pain.

We can look at pain in three categories remembering that each of these are connected.

1. **Physical Pain:** This is pain caused by physical injury, such as falling or breaking a bone.
2. **Emotional Pain:** This is pain caused by upsetting emotions, such as feeling sad, hurt, lonely, etc.
3. **Mental Pain:** This is pain caused by a habit of anxious thinking, judging, begrudging, being self-critical, jealousy, being controlling, or feeling controlled, hurtful words etc.

When we are in pain, we need to be mindful of soothing ourselves and not going on to create more pain for ourselves by seeking lots of attention for our situation, ruminating in our negativity, or engaging in self-harm. When we feel a lot of pain, we need to be mindful of not inflicting pain on others by saying hurtful things or talking negatively.

Don't be self-destructive within yourself. It heightens tension in the body, causing pain.

Be kind, understand yourself, let go, relax, and be calm.

Causes of pain

Headaches may be caused by negative thinking. We feel pain due to feeling strongly that situations are not as we want them to be. Being gentle with ourselves, stretching out tight muscles, taking our control back from others, and letting go of blaming ourselves and others eases headaches.

Chest pain may be caused by worry and not breathing properly, which prevents the circulation from flowing freely in the chest muscles. We can talk to ourselves in a soothing way, practice daily meditation, and breath more deeply to lessen chest pain.

Throat problems may be caused by negative thinking, which restricts self-expression. Speaking our truth honestly and accepting our true identity alleviates throat pain.

Skin Issues may be caused by feelings of irritation or annoyance. Flare-ups in skin conditions are often caused by resentment, anger, and temper. Skin problems are eased by truthfully expressing our feelings and by making time for ourselves in the day to do something we really enjoy. They are also eased by eating less of foods that don't suit our bodies.

Aches in the joints may be caused by avoiding looking at our true selves and being in an angry, destructive state of mind. They are also caused by hiding and suppressing feelings and traumas and storing situations instead of dealing with them.

Period pain is very common. Changing hormone levels and times of transition such as starting secondary school can heighten these emotions and cause negativity, leading to physical pain. In adult life, stored emotions in the womb and ovaries can cause painful periods, and polyps and cysts. Left unresolved, womb and fertility issues can develop over time. Period pain can be relieved by naming and accepting the heightened emotions and also by warmth and comfort.

Pain caused by impact injuries such as a car accident: We can store a lot of suppressed emotion in the skeleton. When we suffer a sudden impact, the body gets rattled, and emotions we have stored away can surface and add to our pain. After an accident, we need time to rest and be looked after. You may need hospital assistance to help mend broken bones and heal internal injuries. If we are still in pain after a reasonable period of healing, we should look at the emotions that the impact has released. Addressing these feelings and gaining clarity will allow the rest of our pain to be released.

Generational pain is a pain that has been handed down to us through the generations. Some families suffer from a weak back, headaches, heart problems, stomach issues, etc. To ease this sort of pain, it is good to step back from blame and regret. Standing back allows you to see that those who handed the pain to you also suffered. Power to release this pain comes from naming the negative feeling that comes with it and bringing its positive into your life. For example, a weak back might have a corresponding feeling of being unsupported and vulnerable. Cultivating a feeling of support and strength will heal the pain. It is especially rewarding to resolve this kind of pain as it prevents it from being handed to the next generation.

Pain Can Move Around the Body

The way we hold our skeleton influences how pain can move around the body. For example, if your right hip has pain, you will naturally walk with less weight on that hip and put more pressure on your left hip, which will cause pain on the left side of your body over time. If you carry lots of tension in your neck, the muscles will tighten, restricting circulation and can cause pain between your shoulder blades which can then move to one shoulder. To release this sort of pain, a sense of curiosity is needed to travel back through the body with it and let it go with the clarity gained at its origin.

How do you deal with pain? Do you try to ignore it? Fight it? Do you go into 'poor me' mode? Do you sit with it and look at it, or do you hide it?

Easing Pain

The key to healing pain is to sit with it. Pain is a call for your attention. What does it want to say? Is it pointing out old negative habits that are limiting you? Is it asking you to release trauma from the body, of something that happened when you were younger, something that you can now face and deal with? Is it asking you to stop thinking negatively and to think and speak kindly and positively to yourself and others? Is it generational pain that you have the power to release so that the suffering in your family ends with you?

Don't allow yourself to worry about the pain. Don't dramatize it and make it bigger. Don't make it your fault. Acknowledge it. It's there, and that is ok. Soften your thoughts. Just sit with the pain and allow it to be. When you sit in this way with a sense of acceptance and non-judgement, you give your pain the attention it needs, and it will transform every time. Look at what emotions the pain represents for you? With this clarity, observe the release of the negativity and let go of some or all of the pain. Imagine white loving light energy coming in to flood the area. Have compassion for yourself. This allows you to relax and ease to return to your body.

> **Journal Exercises**
>
> *What is your experience of pain?*
>
> *Where do you hold pain in your body?*
>
> *Is your pain, physical, mental, or emotional?*
>
> *What emotional blockage do you have that creates your pain?*
>
> *What helps you to deal with the pain?*
>
> *How could you resolve the pain and have more ease in your body?*

Stepping Back - When Migraine Attacks

I was hospitalised with severe migraines when I was twenty-nine during that stressful period in my life, raising a young family with a thousand questions about my marriage which battled against wounds in my inner mind. The muscles constricted around my forehead, circling the top of my head and crushing at the nape of my neck. A swirling nausea left me lightheaded and overly sensitive to the light bouncing off the stark white walls of the hospital. The pain bombarded me along with an incredible assault of thoughts attached to old experiences which had been so tightly compressed in my head. These traumatic memories overwhelmed me.

Not surprisingly, no matter how many vials of blood they took to analyse or how many scans I underwent, the tests couldn't find a cause for these severe headaches. The migraines were relentless, and I couldn't concentrate my attention on raising my boys with the constant swell of pain. The counselling helped as the memories and thoughts took over. For two years, in an attempt to manage and understand the trauma in my past and present, which seemed to forever be at my side as the intensity of the migraines persisted, I talked to my counsellor. The more I talked, the more I understood the link between those suppressed thoughts and emotions with my physical pain.

During this time, a monk who taught in a local secondary school came to our house to hire a bus. As we talked about the weather, our days, and everything in between, he casually mentioned that he could see that I suffered from headaches and wanted to heal my mind. Gently, he placed a hand over my head, and within seconds I could feel the power and surge of energy. This experience was intensely healing and opened the doorway to my own understanding of the gift of healing within me. I never had a severe migraine after that.

I now pause when headaches begin to brood at the top of my spine or over my eyes. I isolate the pressure in my mind and move a surge of energy up through my spine. I ask myself what or who is causing this, and as I find the cause, I bring that information through my head, letting it go while remembering not to over analyse it or let old patterns of thinking take over. I bring in a freer, lighter feeling, connecting with my higher self. Clarity returns to my thinking, and my head feels soothed.

Pain: Key Points to Remember

- Pain can be the result of injury, repressed emotion, or negative thinking being stored in the body.

- In our present culture we tend to disassociate ourselves from the cause of the pain and just look at pain as a physical malfunction. We tend to do all we can to avoid pain by over-relying on pain medication and creating addictions and habits of distraction to avoid feeling what the pain is alerting us to.

- Sitting with pain, giving it our full attention, allows it to open up so that we can acknowledge the deferred emotions and thoughts that we need to look at to transform the energy of the pain and gracefully release, at least some of it from the body.

Chapter Seven

Our Relationship with Food

Food is our source of energy. It maintains our life and gives our bodies fuel for cell creation and growth. It gives our senses wonderful opportunities to experience taste, texture, smell, colour, and a feeling of satisfaction. It nourishes our relationships when we eat together as a family or group of friends. We often use food to help us to regulate our mood and help us deal with our emotions. We may eat some chocolate to give us a lift if we feel low or eat a healthy breakfast to help keep our mood steady in school or work until morning break.

Food and the Use of Food to Suppress Emotion

What sort of relationship do you have with food? How reliant are you on sugar highs and caffeine to cope with your day? Do you see food as nourishment, as a source of comfort, something to feel guilty about, or something you use to control how you feel?

Some people eat quite a bland diet finding it difficult to try new foods. They eat with their eyes and think, "I don't like the look of that." Some of us choose foods based on taste and refuse to eat anything with a strong taste. Others judge food by its texture and refuse to eat something if they think the feel of it in their mouths would be objectionable.

Sometimes we may overindulge, eating beyond feeling full. By doing this, we can use food to push down emotions that we don't want to feel. Sometimes we may feel upset and say we can't eat. This is an attempt to numb our feelings so we don't have to face them. We all have our own relationship with food, and it's valuable to look at it to see the emotional reasons why we sometimes eat in ways that are not the best for our health.

Our relationship with food can get completely out of balance. I have experience of being part of the recovery of some people with anorexia and bulimia. I have also helped a number of people who eat a very limited range of food. The following information constitutes what I have observed while working with people with these difficulties and what I have seen that helped them bring their relationship with food back into balance.

Eating Only White Foods

Some young people only eat a very bland diet of white starchy foods such as white bread, pasta, rice, and potatoes. They find food of other texture, colour, or taste very upsetting, associating these foods with feeling unwell. People who eat this way are highly sensitive and have stored a lot of worry and emotion in their stomachs. When they stick to a white food diet, they can keep their feelings suppressed. Eating white foods helps them to stay with the same predictable pattern of feelings.

Introducing coloured foods and foods that look different, have different textures, or have different tastes releases some stored emotions making them feel sick. They can have stomach cramps, feel nauseous, and overwhelmed with a rush of emotion. They panic, thinking they can't cope with the feeling and try to push it back down.

If you have this difficulty with food, you need to address the emotion stored in the stomach and digestive system. It would be good to have a counsellor guide you through the following:

- Breathe deeply to relax and ground yourself.

- Bring up the emotion that rushes through you when you try to vary your diet. Breathe into it. Name it. Is it a restricted feeling, a horrible feeling, an empty feeling, or a bloated feeling? Do you feel annoyed, agitated, irritable, sad, afraid, or something else? Sit with what comes up and breathe.

- Connect the feeling with a thought. Why do I feel this way? What does this feeling represent for me? What thought was trapped as a feeling in my stomach? Keep breathing deeply, knowing that you are safe and well, and allow the rush of feeling to move through you and out of you so that you are just left with the understanding from the thought.

- Look at the thought. Release the hurt out of it and choose a good feeling to replace it with. Place your hand on your stomach and imagine the good feeling going into your stomach, replacing the old feeling. Breathe gently and acknowledge the well-deserved care that you are giving to yourself.

- Place your attention inside your feet and feel your connection to the earth to ground yourself.

Anorexia

Anorexia can have many causes. In recent times anorexia has become more common in boys as well as girls. The cause for some people is that they feel critical of their physical appearance and feel under pressure to create a certain image. They may create a much-distorted body image, where they see themselves as double the size they actually are when they look in the mirror. They may feel a strong dislike or hate for themselves and their body, and then they start to diet, but it gets out of control, and they starve the body. Some people get lost in this, losing their identity of who they are, which overwhelms them, giving them feelings of being depressed.

Another reason people stop eating is to totally numb their feelings. They can't cope with the amount of hurt and pain they have stored in their body, so they shut down their emotions by shutting down all the body systems. Without food, the natural flow of the body systems is severely restricted. The stomach and intestine stop normal function. For girls, their monthly cycle stops. The chest feels tight. The heart rate becomes irregular, slowing down and speeding up. Thinking clearly becomes difficult as the brain needs nourishment to function correctly, giving the person a sense of depression and anxiety.

Over time a new personality is created in the mind, a controlling, judgemental, negative personality that can feel like a voice in the person's head telling them how awful they are and that they should not eat. The real person can get lost in all of this as they constantly fight the battle between their hunger pain and avoiding the overwhelming sensation of negative emotion.

If you suffer from anorexia, not eating has become an addiction, so recovering from anorexia involves lots of counselling. You may need family or friends to assist you in taking a place in a programme to make a full recovery. Recovery involves opening up and addressing the suppressed feelings, naming the emotions, and releasing the negative thoughts and comments from others stored in your body. You need to take back your power from the negative, cruel personality you have created. Find your self-compassion and self-love. Start to like and value yourself. Find new interests and a purpose for yourself to create a positive future.

Bulimia

Bulimia is an extreme form of binge eating where a person fills themselves up with a large volume of food and makes themselves sick. There is a choking sensation which gives a temporary feeling of relief. They allow themselves the taste of the food but not the nourishment. There is an overfilling of the body and then an emptying of it, right to the bottom of their stomach. It involves feeling a high feeling and a low feeling, and in that sharp swing from high to low, the person can hide from the real feelings they have stored. The body feels unbalanced. Blood sugars rise sharply and crash. The whole system is affected. It can become an addictive behaviour and may be just as serious to the person's health as anorexia.

Resolving bulimia involves a similar course of action to anorexia. If you have bulimia, with the support of counselling and a recovery programme, the questions that will help you make the breakthrough to recovery are, "What do I not want to see? What feelings and thoughts am I hiding from? What disgusts me about myself?" Feeling these emotions with a supportive counsellor, naming them, addressing the thoughts behind these feelings, and replacing them with positive, healing, and kind thoughts will help you break the cycle. Then finding some purpose and excitement about your future will set you securely on the road to recovery.

Recovery from eating disorders takes time. Patience, understanding, love and compassion is needed as often people have hidden the emotions of something traumatic from their past that they have never openly spoken about, something deep-rooted like bullying, the loss of a parent, abuse, etc. If your relationship with food has gotten out of balance, seek support. One good option is *Bodywhys*, a national voluntary organisation supporting people affected by eating disorders.

A Memorable Writing Experience

While writing this section, I asked my guides for help, and the answer was a direct energy connection to people who are currently experiencing eating disorders. We could feel how very unwell they felt in their bodies, the extreme loneliness, the false highs followed by the despairing lows, the impact of the controlling negative voices in their heads, and the need for proper professional help so they can get well. It was exhausting to feel the reality of an eating disorder, but we felt that we were writing something to help the people who need it.

> *Journal Exercises*
>
> *How would you describe your relationship with food?*
>
> *In what way do you use food to regulate your emotions?*
>
> *Do you use food to control or suppress your emotions?*
>
> *What do you need to do to have a healthier relationship with food?*

> **Food: Key Points to Remember**
>
> - It is very interesting to observe our relationship with food, looking at why we eat various foods and when we eat. When we sit with and address our emotional reasons for eating, we are free to focus more on our actual hunger and the nourishment food gives us.
>
> - Sometimes our relationship with food can get very unbalanced. If this happens for you, you will need support from people who have clear insight into the causes of your eating disorder and who are able to help you learn to manage the controlling personality you have created so that you will make a full recovery.

Chapter Eight

Responsibility and Forgiving Others

To be responsible means to be accountable and answerable for yourself, someone else, or something. Responsibility involves carrying some type of emotional, physical, or mental load. It means there are things you are expected to do, manage, or deal with. Take responsibility for yourself and your own words and actions. In your everyday situations, see yourself first and then others.

Even in the hardest circumstances, it is still possible to choose your attitude towards the situation and retain your identity.

By not taking appropriate responsibility, we create one of two difficulties:

We don't take responsibility for ourselves and give away our control over our lives.
When we don't take responsibility for ourselves, we are quick to judge and blame others. When we offload our responsibility, we also give away our power. We do not have control over our own lives. We are putting someone else in the driving seat of our lives and then blaming them for not taking us where we want to go. Take back your

control. Get comfortable with taking responsibility for yourself and looking after yourself. This impacts all areas of your life, your home, family, school, workplace, sport, hobbies, and social life, your present and future.

We take on responsibility for other people, which exhausts us.
Sometimes we carry responsibility for others. Your parents or family members may put a lot of responsibility and expectations on you to be a certain way for them to feel good, for example, to constantly look after the needs of the younger siblings, to achieve high results in school, to behave perfectly, to choose a career in the family business. We can take on the responsibility for our friends' feelings and tie ourselves in knots trying to keep them happy.

Carrying constant responsibility for others is exhausting. The weight of it can wear us out. It can lead us to feel overwhelmed. We feel resentful of others when we do too much to meet their needs and are expected to ignore our own needs. Our thoughts become terribly negative and self-destructive. We can feel unable to manage. Some people become so overloaded with others' opinions, feelings, and responsibilities that they can't cope, and they switch off and opt out of school or work.

We need to hand back other people's responsibility to them. They are responsible for their own feelings, words, and actions. You are responsible for yours. You can manage your own and thrive in your life.

Finding the Balance with Responsibility

- Look at what you take responsibility for. Ask yourself what's yours and what's not yours?

- Take back responsibility for yourself that you have given away.

- Give back responsibility to others for what's not yours. It is good to be kind and to help out family and friends. However, be observant of someone who is putting upon you too much and trying to make you feel obliged to constantly be at their beck and call, to carry what is really their responsibility. Put your boundaries in place.

- Be aware if you or someone close to you tends to act the martyr, taking on too much responsibility and then telling everyone what they are doing and maybe also expecting considerable payback.

- You may have extra responsibility in your life if you have an ill family member, a number of younger siblings, or someone in your family with special needs. If so, sit down with the others involved and put a structure in place so you can agree on exactly what you are responsible for and the times in the week when you will do this, making sure you still have time for your other responsibilities and also time to spend with friends and to do the things you enjoy. This structure will help you do your part without resentment and give you a sense of freedom within your week.

- When you share responsibility with others throughout your life, doing a group project in your workplace, organising an event, or parenting children, practise taking on your fair share of responsibility and learn to respectfully put your boundaries in place if someone is handing their share over to you. Take ownership of yourself.

> *Journal Exercises*
>
> *Do you take responsibility for yourself and your actions?*
>
> *Do you take responsibility for your own decision making? Do you allow others to make decisions for you and then blame them if things don't work out?*
>
> *We need to take ownership of our own actions. What do you need to take ownership of?*
>
> *Do you carry responsibility for others?*
>
> *Do you enjoy or resent taking on responsibility? Look at this question in relation to different areas of your life: partner, parents, siblings, children, grandparents, friendships, work, sport, etc.*
>
> *How does taking on responsibility affect you physically, mentally, and emotionally?*
>
> *What do you need to do to balance responsibility in your life?*

Stepping Back - Growing Up Quickly

Responsibility weighed heavily on me as a child. As the second eldest of thirteen children, I found I grew up a lot quicker than I should have. When I was twelve years old, after the birth of one of my younger siblings, my mother was recovering, and a heavy burden was placed on my young shoulders. A Jesuit priest visited my mother, and as he picked up his coat to leave, he turned to me and told me, with severe conviction, that I was to look after all of my younger brothers and sisters. I couldn't stop crying, yet I also felt I could not go to my recuperating mother with how I was feeling. Headaches persisted because I simply couldn't understand how we would all manage. My father could, at times, get terribly angry, and knowing how this could affect those younger than me, I felt it was my duty to calm him and protect my siblings. So while I cared for them, I was also on high alert for the times I had to talk to our father and soothe his anger. At twelve years old, this was a lot to cope with, and you would imagine it would or should have been a short-lived scenario. However, I carried this burden of responsibility for almost thirty years.

Forgiveness of Others

Forgiveness is a decision we make to let go of the emotional, mental, and physical impact that a situation has had on us. It involves looking at the other person's issues, problems, or viewpoint and understanding where they were at in their lives. We observe them and the impact they have had on us with clarity and then decide for our own benefit to process the issue and let it go. We then take back full responsibility for ourselves and how we act, think, and feel.

Sometimes other people's words and actions can be hurtful. Sometimes we hold onto hurt, hold onto a grudge, or hold onto a thought about what someone did to us. What we find difficult to forgive depends on our life experiences, our views and opinions, our values, and our insecurities. We can let go of some hurts easily and take longer to let go of others depending on the situation.

Sometimes we think that people who hurt us don't deserve to be forgiven. We may have been completely traumatised by the actions of another. The impact of what they did may have had a lasting negative impact on our lives. We may have become attached to playing the victim and gaining sympathy from everyone who will listen to how we were wronged. We may have hidden how we suffered at the hands of another and internalised our pain. We might hold morals and beliefs so rigidly that we have little capacity to tolerate any behaviour that falls below our set standard.

When you refuse to forgive, you feel stuck as you are not letting the situation go. You carry the toxic situation in your body physically as pain, emotionally as uncomfortable feelings, and mentally as repeating thoughts or occasionally triggered thoughts. You could carry experiences in your body for years, which can make you unwell. Some people carry many such situations in their bodies, which causes them a lot of suffering and makes them negative, anxious, and depressed.

How to Forgive

Step back a little from the situation. Stop the judgement. Be open to looking at the situation in a different way. You don't know what was going on in the other person's life that caused them to act as they did. You feel what they have said or done has impacted you, but it's really that you have suffered because of their stored negative emotions, which may have been passed down to them through generations or were caused by their early childhood trauma. Their actions reflect their issues rather than having anything to do with you. People who are feeling secure in themselves don't say or do hurtful things. Realising this does not excuse their behaviour but shows their imperfections as people and makes the impact of what happened less personal.

You also need to forgive yourself. Maybe you are angry with yourself for not keeping yourself safe, for not having your boundaries in place, for allowing yourself to stay too long in a toxic relationship, or for being manipulated by a parent or boss who made you take on too many responsibilities as you tried to gain their approval. Be compassionate with yourself. You may have been too young, vulnerable, physically smaller, or inexperienced to be able to protect yourself. Forgive yourself.

Also, ask yourself what this situation has brought up for you. Can you relate the impact to a feeling you had in the past? Did it trigger a previous hurt that caused your emotions to heighten? Is this an incident that mirrors a primary hurt that is the situation that really needs to be addressed?

- Bring in your new understanding of the situation.

- Sit and acknowledge the impact that holding onto the hurt has had on you and then breathe and decide to let it go for your own benefit.

- Where in your body have you held onto the hurt? Breathe deeply into this area. Visualise the stored hurt opening up and name the feelings there, anger, fear, powerlessness, shame, sadness, etc. Breathe into whatever comes up and allow them to be released out of the body. See the space left being filled with beautiful, coloured healing energy.

- What repeating negative thoughts have you had about yourself because of this experience? Reason with these thoughts reassuring yourself of your worthiness of love and your strengths and value.

- What part of yourself did you lose when this happened? Visualise yourself reaching out and taking back what you lost in this situation. Was it your freedom, sense of safety, self-confidence, voice, enthusiasm, self-acceptance, etc.? Take back full ownership and responsibility for yourself. Take back your control and your belief in yourself. Take back your true identity.

- Speak kindly and compassionately to yourself. Soothe the vulnerability in you to find it easier to let go of the hurt in your future.

Sometimes when we release and clear hurt we have held onto, our physical body can go through a further release, and we may get a cold or an upset stomach. All is well. Practice *The Calm Breath*. Be gentle with yourself. All will clear fully in a short time, and you will be all the better for it. Being able to forgive others frees us from being weighed down by hurt and gives us a lighter feeling and renewed energy for living our lives.

> *Journal Exercises*
>
> *How do you view forgiveness?*
>
> *Who do you need to forgive?*
>
> *What do you need to forgive yourself for?*
>
> *What impact is not forgiving someone having on you emotionally and mentally?*
>
> *Where in your body do you feel it when you keep holding onto hurt, shame, and guilt?*
>
> *How does it feel to make the decision to forgive yourself or others?*
>
> *Is there any ongoing situation in your life that you need to move away from or accept and make peace with?*

Responsibility and Forgiveness: Key Points to Remember

- Responsibility involves taking on an emotional, mental, or physical load of some kind.

- We are in our own power when we take ownership of and responsibility for ourselves, directing our own path through life, and choosing what we wish to take on.

- Sometimes due to life circumstances we take on too much responsibility given to us by other people. We exhaust ourselves behaving in a way that suits others, carrying their pain, soothing their emotions, worrying about their concerns, and taking on their workload.

- We need to put structures and boundaries in place onto the responsibility that we take on in our family, work, friendships, and community so that we keep some time, space, and energy for ourselves.

- Forgiveness is about letting go of the negative impact that someone's words or actions have had on us.

- To do this we can take a step back and viewing the situation with clarity and self-compassion, release the hurt stored in our body along with the accompanying thoughts.

- Next we need to take back both the part of us that we lost at that time and full ownership of ourselves.

Chapter Nine

Trauma

A trauma is an event in our life experience that is too much for us to bear physically, emotionally, and mentally. The event may have involved grief, loss, war, attack, violence, injury, cruelty, injustice, abuse, or anger. Trauma can cause us to have no control over our thoughts, making our body freeze with an overwhelming shock as the trauma hits us. We can't process what is happening, and so our mind may go blank. Our instinct is to escape from the situation. We can't believe what we are experiencing. Our body and brain cannot process the trauma in the moment. We may feel as if something has shattered, and we have left our body. Trauma makes us fragile.

After a little time has passed, we need to process the trauma and release it. However, we may want to avoid addressing it and so instead push it down deep in the body in the hope of never having to face it. We may suppress trauma in the body for years. We may have experienced multiple traumas, which, when unaddressed over time, can cause illness in the body. Some people store trauma so deeply they even lose the memory of it. However, the body still remembers. Some can talk about the trauma but without any emotion because they have disconnected the feelings from the memory.

In the course of our lives, especially during a time of stress, anxiety, grief, or injury, stored trauma can be triggered and heightened. Our brain and body can suddenly alter and go into the mode of the initial impact of the trauma. Our muscles tighten. A puff of shock runs through our body. The shock may bounce around in our body, head, neck, chest, stomach, lower back, and legs, causing physical pain. This can cause sudden changes in mood, irritability, anxiety, phobias, depression, and the creation of personalities. We may feel drained, find it difficult to sleep, be unable to function, feel spaced out, and feel pressure all over our body.

We may, often unconsciously, have a habitual behaviour that we use to put the lid back on our suppressed trauma. This habit is often a coping strategy that we had at the time of the trauma, so it may not be age-appropriate or reflective of our current level of maturity. We may tantrum, eat excessively, pick a row with someone to distract ourselves from the old feelings that are bubbling up, buy things we don't need, create a pattern of illness such as repeated chest infections, experience back trouble, or stomach issues. However, while this habit may help us cope somewhat, it does not resolve or heal the trauma.

Let today be the day you stop holding on to what hurts you and start reaching for happiness.

Addressing the Impact of Trauma

- In what way have traumatic events been experienced by you?
- How have you handled trauma in your life?
- Do you keep reliving the traumatic event?
- Do you create chaos in your life and the lives of others because you have not dealt with your trauma?
- Do you talk to everyone about your trauma, keeping a version of it active in your present but never experiencing the truth of it and moving on in your life?

- Do you avoid it completely, blocking out what happened and its impact on you, keeping yourself away from all triggers that may threaten to bring up memories and feelings that you think you can't cope with?

- What effect does that trauma have on your personality today? Are you defensive and on high alert for threats to your safety?

- Are you shy, and do you hide yourself and your strengths, gifts, and opinions?

- Do you seek conflict or avoid conflict?

- Do you constantly question yourself about what is true?

- Does it affect your hearing because you have learned to disassociate yourself from an unwanted reality?

- Is your clarity of sight affected because you are afraid to see anything that might trigger uncomfortable feelings?

- Have you turned down your ability to feel, to lessen the impact on your life but, in doing so, also limited your capacity to feel joy, passion, and inspiration?

- Do you suffer from chronic illnesses?

- Is one side of your body weaker than the other?

Healing Trauma

The choice is always there for us to let go of the impact trauma has had on us. It is beneficial to our physical, emotional, and mental health to release stored trauma and heal ourselves. To do this, we first need to realise that the triggered emotions are not as real and intense as we think, as they are remembered feelings rather than emotions that belong to the present moment. If we can allow them to surface, we can let them go.

- In times of stress, grief, or injury, what memory or image is triggered in you that causes you distress?

- What habits have you developed to cope with these memories, so you don't have to deal with them fully?

- Resist the urge to follow this habit and instead take some quiet time to look at what memories, feelings, and images are coming up.

- Reassuringly talk to yourself. Tell yourself that it is not happening now and that you are safe and everything is ok.

- Acknowledge your strength and that you survived this situation, and that now you are no longer willing to carry the impact of it around with you in your life.

- Ask yourself, "Where in the body have I locked away this trauma? Where in my brain did I hide it?" Where is the pain of the trauma stored? Let the flow of emotions run through your body without judgement. Stay present. Breathe deeply. Take ownership of your part of the experience. Sit with yourself in a caring way. Acknowledge the trauma. Stay strong in the present as you let the old pain flow out of your body.

- If your trauma was caused by someone else take a moment to acknowledge what was going on with whoever hurt you. Acknowledge the effect their life experiences and childhood had on them and know that they acted from their own pain and insecurity. Talk to yourself and tell yourself that you were not to blame for their actions. Separate yourself from their actions and emotions and visualise giving back to them what does not belong to you.

- The key to healing the trauma is to name the part of you that you lost at that time and age when you felt shattered in the experience and to take back ownership of this part of yourself. Staying strong in the present while acknowledging the past helps you deal with its effect on you now. So what did you lose? Was it your voice, your confidence, and your belief in yourself? Was it your self-respect or sense of worthiness? Was it your sense of safety? Name it. You have been searching for this piece of yourself. Visualise this part of you returning. Take it back. It belongs to you. Take back your power. Feel your strength in owning this piece of yourself again. Breathe into it.

- Regaining your power, independence, and the essence of who you are brings an amazing strength. Breathe in love, joy, and security. Choose a comforting colour to breathe into your body and surround yourself with this colour. Acknowledge the increase in the strength of your connection with your true self. Feel gratitude for what you have given back to yourself. Once you feel that wholeness, you won't give away that part of yourself again.

If you find it difficult to do this on your own, follow a similar process with a counsellor's support. For your future, bring forward in yourself an awareness of who you are and what you want for yourself in life. Set your boundaries for what behaviour you will accept from others and what you will not accept. Know that memories of trauma may still be triggered (in a lesser way) but as you continue to talk soothingly to yourself, let the pain go and empower yourself, the impact of these memories gets weaker and weaker until they no longer bother you. Protect yourself from people and situations that make you feel vulnerable by grounding yourself and using your breath to make and own your space around you.

The strength you gain and the qualities you develop through facing and healing trauma become a profound source of goodness, power, and creativity. The traumatic events that happened no longer hold you, and you are free to pursue your life's goals and dreams.

A Memorable Writing Experience

The preparation for writing this piece was particularly hard on us. I asked questions to my guides about trauma, how it affects us and how to heal ourselves. I quietened my mind to listen to their answer, but an experience was sent rather than words. In a sudden rush, an old traumatic event opened up for each of us, and we felt it afresh as if it had just happened, its effects on us physically and the thoughts and emotions that were running through us. I was told that the key to healing trauma was to name what we had lost in the experience and focus on taking back ownership of that part of ourselves. For me, it was self-respect, and for Susan, it was her voice. There is powerful learning in direct experience. The notes for the topic flowed. At the end of our writing session, my mother and an elderly neighbour of Susan's came in spirit and cleared the remnants of these traumas from our bodies and energy fields, leaving us feeling soothed.

> *Journal Exercises*
>
> *Were you able to recognise trauma and the impact it has had on you?*
>
> *Where in the body have you stored trauma?*
>
> *What part of yourself did you lose in a traumatic event that you need to take back?*
>
> *Which of your strengths and beliefs do you need to acknowledge as you heal from trauma?*

Addiction

Addiction is a created dependency on an activity or substance such as drinking energy drinks, playing console games, using social media excessively, smoking, drinking alcohol, playing violent games, gambling, watching pornography, or taking drugs. Some addictions are much more potentially harmful than others.

People are addicted to things to create a feeling. They get a buzz or a high. These feelings, though, are false feelings that temporarily mask the true feelings underneath, that the person wants to avoid. These feelings are often linked to anxiety, trauma, or depression. Through addictions, a person's reality feels altered. There is confusion about what is true. People can lose the structure of their lives. Their identity feels distorted. People can opt-out of social interactions and isolate themselves. They can feel a lot of guilt and lose their self-worth.

Those who are seriously addicted lose their control, trust, faith, and belief in themselves. They start to look for bigger highs to counteract the lows and create further chaos in their lives.

We pick up habits as we grow up, some good, some bad. Learn from the good and let go of the bad habits. They don't serve you well. Acknowledge the positives in your life.

Solving Addictions

If you are suffering from addiction, seek help. Addictions are easier to solve at a young age, but there is always time. Ask for help from a trusted friend and organise counselling. To let go of the addiction, you need to understand why it is there, create a plan to let go of it, and recover your true identity. To help with managing addiction, see a list of supports available in the resources section.

Preventing Addictions

When you feel an impulse or compulsion to repeat a behaviour, look at how you are feeling. All feelings you desire are available. There are better ways to get to the feeling, ways that won't damage your physical, emotional, and mental health, your relationships and your future best life. Learn to challenge compulsive thoughts. Compulsive thoughts come from a created personality. Stand strong in your real self. Take back your power and true identity. Take charge of the situation and reason with the false personality. You need to become aware of and then break the habits you have created around your addictive behaviours. You need to find a positive outlet to replace the behaviour, such as exercise.

> *Journal Exercises*
>
> *Do you have an addiction? If so, what is your addiction?*
>
> *How impulsive are you?*
>
> *What feeling comes up just before you engage in addictive behaviour?*
>
> *What emotions are you trying to suppress?*
>
> *What truth are you hiding from?*
>
> *How would you rate your highs and lows on a scale of 1-10?*
>
> *How difficult is it to manage your addiction?*
>
> *Can you admit to others that you have an addiction and get the help that you need to resolve it and its underlying cause?*

Healing the Inner Child: Healing trauma and upset that occurred in childhood

Healing the inner child is about healing things that happened that upset us when we were younger. Many of us had experiences we did not fully process in our early years because we couldn't cope with the situation at that young age. This can result in us storing uncomfortable thoughts and feelings in our body. Most of the time, we are not even aware we carry this pain around in our body. However, every so often, something happens in the present that triggers those suppressed emotions and pain. We can feel confused by an overreaction of anger, sadness, fear, self-doubt, or rejection. When we notice this happening, we can make a mental note to find a quiet time to sit down and address the issue.

Our valuable life experience and advanced maturity now means we can go back with the skills to support the younger version of ourselves to navigate our way through these events. Once we have addressed the situation and released the stored thoughts and feelings, we can then allow the memory to place itself in its proper place in the past. It will stop impacting us unexpectedly in everyday life because the trigger has been deactivated.

How to heal the inner child

Sit quietly and take a few deep, slow breaths. Imagine white light beneath your feet and visualise it moving into your feet, going up into your legs, into your knees, pelvis, hips, stomach, into all the organs of the body, up the hands, arms, shoulders and into the chest, heart and lungs, throat and up out through the top of your head. Visualise a ball of light at the base of your spine. Allow it to shine very brightly and then move up your whole spine, pulling you together. Take back your control, trust, self-belief, and faith in your potential and in the support that is there for you.

- Bring yourself into your time, here and now. Feel present in your body.

- Be aware of your life experiences and strengths to date. Everything that has happened along the way has value. Be gentle with yourself.

- Think about the issue that came up for you. Give yourself time. Sit with the feelings that surprised you and acknowledge them.

- Ask yourself, "Where do I need to go back in my life to heal the younger me?" What memory and what age comes up for you? Visualise a white screen. Place it at a comfortable distance in front of you. Stay in the present and play a movie of the situation that needs healing.

- Move closer and look at the effect the situation has on you, as the child on the screen. Then feel the emotions of your child self in your body. What words would you use to describe how the younger you feels? Take your time. Ask yourself what did your inner child need to cope with this situation? Acknowledge that through your maturity, you are now able to heal the younger you.

- Visualise yourself getting down, to eye level, with your inner child to give them what they need. Perhaps it's clarity about what happened and which parts of the situation belonged to others, a hug, love, encouragement, reassurance, positive words, or whatever you feel is appropriate. Reassure yourself that you, the older version of you, is there for them. Tell the younger you about the strengths you now have and give them the gift of the feeling, quality, or strength that you know they needed at that time.

- Acknowledge knowing that this child is always part of you. Thank 'younger you.'
- Come back to the present. Notice what has changed in how you feel in your body.
- Become aware of your body. Be aware of the left and right sides of your body? Do you feel balanced? Which part of your body needs more healing? Tune into this area and bring in green healing light. Visualise the light strengthening this part of your body. Next, allow the energy to flow into the pelvis, lower abdomen, upper abdomen, chest and heart, throat, head and out through the top of your head, connecting with your spiritual connection. Then visualise energy flowing back down through the top of your head, down through your body and out through the bottom of your feet, anchoring you into the ground.
- Take a few moments to breathe and stretch out the body.

Grief

Those who leave us are never far away from us.
They are by our side. Look for the signs.

Grief is an overwhelming emotion and trauma. When we lose a life partner, parent, grandparent, sibling, or friend, we profoundly miss our connection with this person. The emptiness is difficult to bear. The death of a loved one can hit us extremely hard, like a blow that pushes us back into ourselves. We don't feel fully present in our body. We can go into a trance-like state. We can't believe what is happening. It just doesn't feel real that our loved one is gone. For some time after, we may feel transparent, like we are just existing, going through the motions with no spark or enthusiasm. We need time to re-adjust to life without their physical presence.

Grief is a process that can bring up a huge number of feelings such as trauma, shock, disbelief, panic, sadness, blame, anger, regret, anxiety, a sense of unfinished business, fatigue, depression, guilt, fear about our future, and so much more. Processing such an overload of emotion can lead to feelings of isolation and a sense that no one understands what we are going through.

When someone we love passes, we feel the insecurity of them not being there. Compounding this feeling of vulnerability is that other people that we love and depend on may be very shaken by the loss of this person too, and we can feel for a time that our support structure is unsteady. The security of the whole family unit can be hit, and everyone deals with their grief in different ways and over different time scales.

Expression of grief varies from person to person. Some will constantly talk about their loss, and others won't express it openly at all. Some will start dealing with their grief immediately, and others will seem to cope very well with it at first but will be floored by it after a month, six months, a year, or two years. There are also a number of people who seem to deal with grief relatively easily and accept the loss quickly, and life continues quite normally for them. If the family unit had unresolved issues with each other or with the person who has passed, these issues are likely to heighten. There can be a lot of anger, irritation, upset, sadness, and difficult memories coming up. When the family needs to rally and support each other, people may have disagreements.

Sometimes grief is totally overwhelming, like when a loved one takes their own life, when a child dies, when the person who dies was the person we loved the most. We may experience the loneliness of the incompleteness of a promised relationship, as when a parent dies too young or a baby is lost through miscarriage or stillbirth. The pain can be too extreme to bear. We may shut down emotionally and stay numb for a while because it is all too much.

Grief tends to come in waves like the sea, in big waves that go over our head, overwhelming us and small waves that tug on our heart. At the start, waking up and remembering they are gone can hit us with anguish. Seeing their everyday belongings, clothes, books, etc., can floor us. We can feel a physical ache in our heart. We may feel grief as a jolt to the stomach. It takes time for our logical brain to accept that when we look over where we would usually see our loved one, they are not physically there. Our thoughts can race about how we will cope with our new future bringing up intense anxiety. Bit by bit, as time passes, the frequency of the larger waves of grief lessen. Birthdays, Christmas, family occasions such as weddings continue to be tinged with a sense of loss but gradually become times of joy.

The Fallout of Death

Grief has a way of opening up emotions we have suppressed in the body. During the time of more intense grief, when we are trying to come to terms with our loss, we are vulnerable. Unresolved issues and memories we have suppressed can surface and add to our feelings of grief.

Sometimes it can be complicated if the relationship we had with the person we lost wasn't straightforward. The person may have had significant faults or been awfully hard to mind close to their death. We may have had a significant row with them that was unresolved. We need to separate the shared love and the good memories from the other issues so we know what to hold onto and what to resolve and release. A few sessions with a good counsellor can support us as we navigate our way through everything coming up. Letting overwhelming feelings build up and choosing not to get help can lead to ongoing anxiety or depression.

After the loss of a family member, it takes time for that person's legacy to settle in the family. What treasures did the person bring to the family unit? Were they the listening ear, the wise one? Did they have a quiet presence that steadied the family? Did they gather everyone together for meals and chats? Did they bring spontaneity and a sense of humour, and fun? Did they point out to others their true identity and strengths? What did their life teach the family? Through their life, what did you learn is important? What issues had they not yet mastered? Watch their legacy trickle down through the family as people take on their roles and strengths as well as continuing to resolve their struggles. This is all part of the grieving process.

The material possessions a person leaves behind can cause rifts in families. It is great if a will has been made and everyone involved knows its content so that property and money can be distributed according to the person's wishes without any surprises. Some people can be harsh and money-grabbing when a family member dies, and it is sad to see people falling out over not getting what they imagine they have a right to. Such conflict is difficult and unnecessary. It is also an ease for families if loved ones who are dying make their funeral wishes known. It prevents uncertainty and worry about what the person's wishes would have been.

How to Heal

- Acknowledge your loss. Acknowledge you have lost someone and that you need to be compassionate with yourself while you learn to come to terms with a new reality.

- Know that it is okay to be upset. It's okay to cry.

- Regularly take time to sit quietly and feel the emotions that are coming up for you. Look at yourself in a caring way. Don't push away the emotions. You need to feel your loss and own your grief. Create a circle of support for yourself and frequently explain to someone who loves you how you feel. As you feel and name your emotions and allow yourself to be supported, you can move through the grief. If you feel you are getting stuck and can't see your way through all of the thoughts and feelings coming up, seek some added support from a grief counsellor.

- Don't judge your feelings. You will have good days and difficult days. You can't predict how you will feel after someone's passing.

- Give yourself time and space to recover. Take some time away from work or school and reduce your number of commitments.

- Take time to sit and remember the good memories, the treasures of your relationship. Talk about the happy times. Frame some photos of these memories or make an album. Own each of these memories and bring them forward with you into your future as a source of happiness and strength.

- Remember the learning this person gave you, the strengths you have developed because of your relationship with them and feel gratitude for your relationship. Do something to express your gratitude and to honour their relationship with you.

- While your loved one is no longer here in the physical world, the love between you still exists. Regularly sit, place your hand on your heart and tune into the presence of your shared bond. Feel their love and comfort flowing to you. Often when someone you love passes, you feel some part of yourself is gone with them. For example, if you had a similar sense of humour, you may find it hard to see the fun in things anymore, or if they were good at organising things, you might feel incapable of sorting anything out. You need to take some time and check-in with yourself to see what part of you is missing and then breathe deeply and call it back to yourself. Imagine this piece of you coming down from above your head and landing softly into your body where it belongs. Take ownership of this important part of you. Also, remember to take back any of your control that you had given to this person. Taking back and owning these parts of your identity gives you power. It will add to your energy levels, help you cope more easily, and feel better emotionally.

Take back your control, trust, belief, and faith within yourself. Know that you will get through this time of grief and that while your life is changed due to the loss of your loved one, you can cope, and you will enjoy life again.

A Memorable Writing Experience

We had decided to finish our work for the evening, both emotionally exhausted after opening up our own grief and the feelings of the different kinds of grief that you, our reader, might go through to write this piece. Simultaneously our attention was drawn into the centre of the living room. We could both sense a tall presence, angelic in nature, connecting to us, heart to heart. This angel radiated unconditional love to us, flooding us with love and support. There was a soft feminine quality to the energy. We could also sense my dad and Susan's uncle there to lend us their support. After the presence faded, we were still physically tired, but our grief had been washed away. It is a treasured experience, one that reassures us that always in the bigger picture, everything is okay.

> **Journal Exercises**
>
> *What is the cause of your grief?*
>
> *How would you describe grief?*
>
> *How does it make you feel? Do you carry it in your head or your body?*
>
> *Does some of the grief you are carrying actually belong to someone else?*
>
> *Who do you need to talk to in order to help you cope with your grief?*
>
> *Will you bring this grief into your future?*
>
> *Do you need to take back your control from someone who has passed?*
>
> *Are you being gentle with yourself as you process your loss?*
>
> *What do you need to do more of to help you to deal with grief?*

Bullying

Bullying is a form of manipulation where a person persistently seeks control of another, creating underlying trauma. Bullying can be verbal or physical. Social media platforms such as Facebook, Instagram, Snapchat, and TikTok can be misused as a tool for bullying and make life exceedingly difficult for a person being bullied, as the harassment is relentless.

> *The struggles you see today develop into the strengths that make you a strong person. Courage is what it takes to stand up and speak for yourself.*

Why do People Bully Others?

People bully because they are jealous, and they feel insecure when they compare themselves with others. Some people bully to be noticed and to get attention. Bullying behaviour often stems from early childhood experiences of feeling insecure. As a child, the bully may have learned that fighting is the way to get noticed and get their way at home. They may have been verbally abused and accused of not being good enough. They may have been bullied by someone older in the family. They may have had to take on responsibilities that were beyond their coping skills. They then bullied as a way of expressing a build-up of anger and resentment. They picked on others in school or the workplace, often the more sensitive person or someone they perceive to be the group leader, to offload their lack of security and feel powerful.

Often, the person who bullies wants to get in with a group and appear cool or gain a leadership position within a group. They want others to see that they have authority. They enjoy having a sidekick or two to inflate their feelings of importance, which can lead to a threatening group. People bully to try to free themselves of their fear of being judged. They want the power to manipulate people whom they perceive to be a threat. People who bully can become very skilled at twisting and manipulating situations to justify their actions.

What are the Effects on the Person Being Bullied?

The impact of being bullied varies greatly from person to person. It depends on the severity of the bullying and the length of time it goes on. It depends on the level of sensitivity of the person being bullied and on the level of support the person feels they have in their life. Support is based on trust from both their family and friends and whether or not they can confide in someone about what is going on.

Being bullied can be devastating. It can make a person feel vulnerable, embarrassed, and isolated. Being bullied has a negative impact on health, quality of sleep, and outlook. It can make people question their self-worth and their personality. Their thoughts can be very fearful and self-critical. Without emotional support and an effective plan to stop the bullying, the bullied person can feel powerlessness and despair.

How to Cope with Being Bullied

- Learn to create clear boundaries. If you feel you are easily led or manipulated, you need to learn to stand back from situations, look clearly at what is going on, and see if the person's motives are genuine. Practise speaking with confidence and stating your intentions clearly. Have some statements ready for your protection, such as,

  "That doesn't suit me."

  "I don't like this situation and where it's going."

  "This makes me uncomfortable."

  "I don't want to do this right now."

  "I need time."

  "I disagree."

  Be prepared to walk away from situations.

- If you are being bullied, tell people you trust, such as friends, family members, a teacher if it is happening in school or a colleague at work. Sometimes this can be hard, especially if the person bullying you threatened to reveal something that embarrasses you if you tell. Don't give them that power; tell people you trust. They will understand. Tell in detail what has been happening and exactly how you are feeling. Do not keep everything to yourself. Let the people who support you help you create a plan for the future, a plan to stop the bullying, and help you recover.

- Know that this is not your fault. The person who bullies does it because of what is going on with them. Understanding this will help you take a step back, view the situation from a larger perspective, and not take what is happening as personally.

Solving Bullying Behaviour

It can often be difficult to encourage the person who bullies to take responsibility for their behaviour and change. Loss of friendships, when others set their boundaries and decide that the bully's behaviour is unacceptable, can provide a window of vulnerability whereby the person who bullies might see that their behaviour is also causing themselves pain. Counselling is needed to give the person clarity on why they bully and to take ownership of the hurt they have caused. They need a lot of support to face their insecurities and heal the hurt so that they no longer feel the need to control, manipulate, and hurt others.

If the person who bullies is unwilling to change their behaviour, then it is up to the wider community in school or the workplace to stand up and lend their strength to support people who are being bullied as the bully's power evaporates when their victim no longer feels weak or isolated.

> *Journal Exercises*
>
> *What do you see as bullying behaviour?*
>
> *Describe the personality of a bully?*
>
> *Have you acted as a bully?*
>
> *If so, have you addressed why you did this and resolved this behaviour?*
>
> *Have you been bullied?*
>
> *If so, how did it affect you?*
>
> *Have you spoken about it?*
>
> *Do you feel isolated? What support do you need?*
>
> *What are your boundaries?*

Feeling Safe

It is safe for you to speak up for yourself.
Take back your control, trust, faith, and belief in yourself.
Be one with you.

Feeling safe means we do not expect hurt or harm, either physically or emotionally. We feel secure in ourselves and know that we can manage what the day will bring and enjoy our life.

Feeling insecure and unsafe can come from:

- A fear of facing difficult situations in the present.
- A fear of being judged and of not being able to be true to yourself.

- Unrealistic expectations from your partner, family, and friends.
- Suppressed emotions and a fear of being unable to cope when these feelings are triggered.
- A fear of physical, emotional, mental or sexual abuse.

Cultivating a feeling of safety and of feeling protected:

- Does your home give you a sense of safety?
- Do you feel safe at school or work?
- Do you feel secure in yourself, valuing yourself, and settled in your own body and personality?
- Which family members, teachers or work colleagues help you to feel safe?
- Have you found friends that suit you, with whom you feel confident and at ease?
- Does the routine of your day give you a sense of safety?

When you identify the areas of your life that give you a sense of security and safety, focus on these as a basis for building a stronger sense of safety.

Build your internal sense of safety by:

- Reassuring yourself of your own value.
- Having an awareness of your thoughts and recognising when they create a feeling of worry or judgement. Have compas-

sion for yourself and infuse your thoughts with hope and optimism.

- Doing something every day that gives you a feeling of safety, such as chatting to someone kind who knows you well, curling up on the couch with a good book, walking your dog, or playing music.

- In some circumstances, it is not easy to see a way out. If you feel trapped or isolated, you need to seek help from a trusted friend or counsellor to help you plan a way out of the situation and build a new future for yourself. You can then build up your belief in yourself, take back your self-worth, and take ownership of yourself. See the resources section at the end of the book for a list of supports available to you.

What to do when you witness something upsetting:

Observe how you react:
- Do you tend to feed into things and become part of the drama, or do you stay out of it?
- Do you excessively worry about those involved?
- Do you often over-react and add to the situation?

You can change the effect of seeing this situation because what you are feeling is mostly not yours. Don't own it. The feelings belong to the people involved. Clear your body and give back the feelings to whom they belong. Bring in a positive feeling. If someone is very vulnerable in the situation, seek help for them.

> *Journal Exercises*
>
> *How safe do you feel within yourself?*
>
> *How would you describe feeling safe?*
>
> *Do you feel protected?*
>
> *Do you put unrealistic expectations on yourself?*
>
> *What kind of structure do you have in your life? (Family, home, friends, daily routine, school, work, activities, leisure time, screen time, sleep patterns, etc.)*
>
> *What do you need to do to build up your sense of safety?*

Stepping Back - The Bully Trauma

Our school days can be memorable for the right and the wrong reasons. My memories, at one stage, were overloaded by recollections of a few children in my class who taunted me. As they shouted hurtful names and teased me, I would squeeze my hands tightly, wishing so hard to be smaller and less noticeable so the bullies would forget I was there and leave me alone.

But, of course, I couldn't blend away, and some of them continued to pick on me until my nervousness amplified. That feeling of being self-conscious ignited a stammer that ultimately made me stand out more and gave them another reason to find fault. Their jarring comments made me shrink away in the classroom, and when called upon by teachers, I struggled to find the words.

Those years were fraught with tension, and I was heavily insecure about my heightened sensitivities as I was not at a place in my life yet to work through the emotions these bullies brought up in me. Those emotions became stuck and were deeply embedded, blocking my energy and ability. Through my inner child healing work, I began to focus on seeing with clarity the insecurities of those who were name-calling. Through practice, I released their negativity stored in my body and reassured my younger self, soothing any self-doubt. Over time, I taught myself to speak slowly, break the words down, and let my speech flow more freely. I regained my voice. I owned my voice. When I speak in front of large groups of people with my healing work, I am so pleased with how far I have come.

> **Trauma: Key Points to Remember**
>
> - A trauma is an event whose impact was too distressing for us to process at the time it happened.
>
> - The key to healing trauma is to allow the stored emotion to come up and flow through our body, to name what we lost at the time, to visualise ourselves taking this aspect of ourselves back, and to own this piece of ourselves again.
>
> - Addictions are created to produce a high feeling in order to find relief from the true feelings underneath.
>
> - If you have an addiction, it's best to work with an addiction counsellor to uncover the causal issue and feelings and to put an effective recovery plan in place.
>
> - If the trauma occurred in childhood it helps to visualise revisiting the experience and talking to the younger you, giving yourself clarity, support, compassion, and love.

- The sadness of grief can be very difficult to deal with. We have to come to terms with the physical absence of someone we loved. We also need to process our relationship with them finding ways to honour this while caring for ourselves. We can find comfort in feeling our connection to their loving presence when we think of them.

- Bullying can cause significant trauma. It leads to us feeling very vulnerable and isolated as it can eat away at our self-confidence.

- To recover from being bullied we need to create our boundaries, seek support until we find sufficient help, and always know that it is the bully who is at fault.

- To feel safe we can focus on reassuring ourselves of our inherent value, keep our thoughts infused with hope, incorporate activities that give us a feeling of safety in our day, and obtain help if we find ourselves in an unsafe situation.

- See the menu of supports in the resource section. One or more of these could help you as you process trauma, addiction, grief, or bullying or if you need to create a safe home environment for yourself.

Chapter Ten

Personalities

Our true nature is to be honest, kind, caring, wise, and loving. We are naturally full of unconditional love, joy, peace, understanding, empathy, fun, excitement, creativity, and optimism. We have self-respect. We feel our worthiness. We nurture our gifts and then share them with others.

As babies, we take the world in through our senses, how we smell, taste, hear, see, and touch, and we also sense the emotions of our mother, father, and others around us. We are all born with different sensitivities, and in this way, we make our own likes and dislikes known. Our parents and guardians responded to these sensitivities making the bond between us deepen as best they could. As we developed in their care, we learned to communicate, crawl, walk, talk, and behave in particular ways. We learned about family structure and relationships, and as we started school, our range of life experiences expanded.

Based on your sensitivity, throughout life, you have tuned into different thoughts and emotions and therefore had a childhood with a vastly different experience from anyone else, even siblings. Sometimes situations arise in life which can bring up pain or unwanted emotions, emotion we don't want to feel. To cope, we tune out and disconnect from the present. As a result, based on our learning to that point in life, we may start forming personalities or greatly amplify an aspect of ourselves to manage and fit in. Though these created personalities can come with benefits at the time, they also come with a price.

When we understand and accept our true selves, we gain strength, courage, and confidence to live life in the present.

Created Personalities:

The Minder - The minder looks out for other people and makes sure they are ok. They help out, share, and nurture others. Minders often give more than what they are comfortable with to fulfil their role. Minders feel a sense of importance from taking on the role of minding; however, they can do too much for others at their own expense. They can lose a sense of their own identity and worthiness and feel resentful of the amount of their time and energy that they give away.

The Pleaser - The pleaser says what they know other people want to hear. They won't rock the boat, always agreeing. Pleasers try to fit in, but they often do so simply to avoid conflict because they don't want to upset others. In this way, pleasers can feel uncomfortable in themselves when they hide who they really are. It is very tiring going around pleasing others, and they often feel exhausted and unseen.

The Bully - The bully wants to be in control and can choose sensitive people to intimidate. Bullies feel weak and insecure in themselves and want to have a sense of authority. More often than not, the bully was persecuted by others in the past. The bully enjoys a sense of power, which can soothe their fear of being judged or feeling vulnerable. They give up their chance for nourishing relationships and true friendships with people. They feel disconnected and on the outside of groups. They also know that their source of power depends on others giving away their control and so is not real.

The Exaggerator - The exaggerator adds more to information than what is true. They tell either the best or worst story, full of drama. When they exaggerate about other people and gossip, their words can cause a lot of hurt. The exaggerator gets a lot of attention from the people who listen to their stories. The exaggerator feels they are not enough in themselves, and their truth is not interesting enough without embellishment. They can be fearful of being found out. Their exaggerations can cause hurt when they speak badly of others. Exaggerators may not be believed by others even when they speak truthfully.

The Withdrawer - The withdrawer does not stay present. They zone out and are not really here. They are not concentrating or focusing with consistency. The withdrawer is not listening to what is going on around them. They disconnect during difficult situations and withdraw into themselves. They avoid having to feel the impact of what is going on around them. The withdrawer misses out on a lot of positive interactions with people and positive emotions because they have shut themselves down. They are often highly sensitive people with wonderful gifts to share, missing out on developing these abilities.

The Shy Person - Shy people do not like to speak or act without a lot of prior thought. They do not like to be put on the spot or challenged. Shy people create a cocoon for themselves, trying to keep their world small and safe. They avoid being questioned and judged. Uncomfortable in groups, they avoid being in the situation of saying the wrong thing. Shy people do not give themselves the freedom of expression. They can get stuck in a lack of self-confidence and feel unworthy. Shy people miss out on a lot of enjoyable life experiences.

The Manipulator - Manipulators want to be in control. They feel jealous of people they perceive as popular and are insecure. They set out to divide people by carrying stories or fibbing. They twist what others have said and like setting people against each other. They often tell secrets, carry stories and gossip. Manipulators stand back and enjoy watching the effect of their destructive behaviour play out. Manipulators get a sense of power by creating negative scenarios. They enjoy creating chaos and bad feeling between others. Manipulators lose out on having true, close friendships and feeling proper connections with people. They isolate themselves by playing people off each other. They create confusion in themselves about what is true and what is not.

The Worrier - The worrier carries a multitude of different anxious thoughts. Their brain gets overloaded. As more anxious thoughts accumulate, they can feel out of control. Worriers may feel sick in their stomachs, sweat excessively, have aches and pains, and feel extremely tired. They usually try to fix other people's worries and are so overwhelmed they can't deal with their own fears. The worrier feels they are making the future safer for themselves by thinking through all possible future scenarios and about how they would cope with each possible situation. They waste a huge amount of energy overthinking and feeling the resulting physical and mental pain. They can suffer from chronic fatigue. Worriers miss out on a lot of the joy in their lives.

The Angry Person - This is a person who is easily angered, offended and is suspicious of the motives of others. They hold on to a lot of emotions and are unable or unwilling to sort, manage, or release these. Holding onto all these feelings exhausts them and significantly reduces their ability to cope with everyday life. They frequently lash out at others verbally or physically. The angry person can get a sense of power from intimidating others. They can feel less vulnerable by keeping people at a distance. They can release an over-accumulation of emotions in outbursts which gives them a temporary sense of relief. The angry person keeps people at a distance and is often lonely and feels depressed. They can suffer from a lot of physical pain and illness due to all the emotions they store in their bodies. They miss out on a lot of good in life by ruminating on the past and thinking the worst of people. They can damage relationships with people they care about by letting their anger get out of control, and some feel a lot of remorse and guilt for their actions.

The Defeatist - The defeatist is afraid of failure, and they decide not to try. They have a wish to be perfect. Defeatists compare themselves to others and opt-out if they think they will not match or better another's achievement. They make up excuses about why they can't do things and make others feel sorry for them. The defeatist protects themselves by not having to face challenges. The defeatist creates poor self-esteem and a negative spiral of thinking for themselves. They are self-destructive, preventing themselves from reaching their potential.

The Joker - The joker likes to make others feel good by acting out. In any scenario, they can make fun and humorous comments. They avoid addressing the issue at hand. The joker is uncomfortable with silence and feels under pressure to perform. They avoid having to make decisions or express their true opinions. The joker gets to avoid being vulnerable and feeling judged. Their true personality is hidden, and even their close friends don't really get to know them which can be lonely. Staying too long in this personality can cause the joker to lose their sense of their own identity. They can be prone to depression.

As you deal with your past, it will benefit you to clarify if and why you created certain personalities. At certain times in your life, these personalities helped you cope with life events, but they have now outlived their purpose. Become aware of when you switch into a false personality. Acknowledge the negative price you pay for each one. Gradually let them go.

What occurs is a feeling of presence to who you really are. There is an honesty and a sense of self-acceptance of the real you. Without putting up a front or putting on a show, who are you? It's about your true instincts of who you are. Your true self feels like an inspiration that rises in you. There is a sense of freedom, power, and belonging. In this space, you feel whole, complete, and worthwhile. You know that you are okay. You speak with clarity, honesty, and kindness. As you accept yourself, you then have great empathy and compassion. Be your true self. Focus on your growth and work towards your potential. Be your own person.

> *Journal Exercises*
>
> *Which personalities have you created to help you cope?*
>
> *Which of these personalities come forward most frequently in your life?*
>
> *What caused you to create these personalities?*
>
> *How often do you switch into a personality that is not true to who you really are?*
>
> *What is your true personality?*

If You Don't Like Yourself

If you don't like yourself, you experience a lot of anger, sadness, inner turmoil, and emotional pain. If you experience not liking yourself for a long time, this may lead to you not looking after yourself properly or, even more distressing, engaging in addictions or self-harming behaviours as a way of trying to deal with or release some of your pain. You may get ill due to the amount of negativity you are holding in your body resulting from your own thoughts or negativity that you have taken on from other people.

However, when you don't like yourself, it is actually a distorted image of yourself that you don't like, rather than your real self. So, don't give yourself a hard time! You have believed a build-up of your own and others negativity and created a distorted view of yourself. It's time to be brave and hold your opinion of yourself up to the light.

You may have created false personalities to avoid facing what is really going on with you. Maybe you have become overly dramatic, creating an upset to get others to pander to your needs, living on the energy of their attention rather than being powerful in your own energy. Perhaps you have opted out of social situations, your studies or work. You may have felt genuinely down and upset but have now gotten yourself stuck behind a self-created depressed personality? Are you using this personality to avoid taking responsibility for yourself? If you have created personalities, you need to look behind the illusion to find your true self. Take ownership of yourself. Stop comparing yourself to others. Let go of the imagined expectations of friends. Stop portraying a false image. You will feel comfortable with and enjoy being who you really are. You will feel light-hearted, relaxed, interested in life, and clear-headed.

To move from not liking yourself to feeling the essence of who you really are, you need to sit with yourself and go deep within, behind the struggle you have created. Ask yourself:

- Who am I, really?

- What resonates with who I really am?

- What activities give me a feeling of flow, a feeling of being in the zone, immersed and energised?

- Am I judgemental of myself and others?

- Which people do I feel comfortable around?

- What are my dreams for me? What small steps can I take in their direction?

- What's false in my life?
- Did something happen to me that I need to get help to heal?
- What strengths and values do I need to take ownership of?
- What have I avoided taking responsibility for?
- What works for me in my life?
- Who do I need to take my control back from?

If you do not like yourself, it is only because you have forgotten your power and identity, the love you have to give, and the love that's there for you to receive. You have forgotten you have a choice and dreams to follow and that everything is ok. Value your worth and reinstate your confidence and self-esteem. Bring out your good qualities and use them.

> *Journal Exercises*
>
> *In what distorted ways do you look at yourself?*
>
> *What do you need to take back to regain your worth?*
>
> *What are your likes and dislikes?*
>
> *What are your talents?*
>
> *What are your unique and best qualities?*

Meditation on Looking at Self

Note: Your energy field is your life-force energy which moves in layers around and through your body. It has four layers: a physical layer closest to the body, an emotional layer, a mental level, and a spiritual one.

To begin this meditation to look at your inner self, close your eyes and relax as you breathe in and out. You are in the here and now. Feel your body sitting in the chair as you take in a few deep breaths. Take in one deep breath, hold it, and let it out nice and gently. Relax your lungs and chest and let your breath go deep into your stomach. Take in another breath, hold it, and let it out nice and gently. Relax your breathing within the rhythm of your heart.

- Become aware of your head. How does it feel? Does it feel light or heavy? Is it negative or full of thoughts? Allow your mind to become clear, don't analyse thoughts, don't question, and don't worry. Just allow thoughts to float in and out of your mind. Allow you to be your true self.

- As you sit with self, become aware of how your head fills up again with thoughts and allow them to filter and clear through your head. How do you feel inside your head? Are you aware of heaviness, dizziness, pressure, pain, memory loss, or stress? Whatever the sensation, acknowledge it and let it go. Allow your head to become lighter and lighter.

- Become aware of your throat. Do you clear your throat? Do you cough? What do you express or not express? Imagine expressing yourself in a loving and caring way without question or doubt. Allow your throat to expand. Allow the inner voice, the voice of truth, to become strong within you. Allow your voice to become one with you.

- Become aware of your chest and lungs as you breathe in and out, allowing your chest to expand. Does your chest feel tight or panicky? Are you breathing comfortably? Do you experience breathlessness, sweating, or emotions rising? Whatever it is, allow it all to clear now. Clear through the chest area.

- Allow your energy to heighten as you move into the heart. Allow the heart to expand. The heart has three layers that need care. Your heart pumps in the moment, in the atmosphere of emotions you pick up from present situations. It pumps in the past of old emotions you've stored, such as hurt, rejection, grief, sadness, and anxiety. It pumps in the influence of your family and the generations who have preceded you. Your heart is affected by unprocessed emotional patterns. Breathe in and then clear all that needs to be released from your heart.

- Move your attention now into the abdominal organs and become aware of this area as you sit with self. You might feel pressure, cramps, or nausea. Visualise your stomach and all the abdominal organs. Become aware of your circulation, muscles, and bones in this area. Allow whatever you need to clear to be released.

- Allow your energy to heighten again. Bring in a feeling of protection around you, visualising a beautiful healing light surrounding you. Choose a soothing colour. This healing light will heal your body. Allow the light to move into the top of your head, lighting up the brain and spinal cord, healing those tissues. Observe the light moving down through the face, throat, chest, heart, lungs, stomach, pelvis, and all the organs in the body.

- Focus on an area three inches below your belly button. Here is the source of your gut feelings, your intuition and knowing, which gives you wisdom and courage in your life. Tune into any influence you have absorbed that you need to clear. Allow it to leave you as you breathe into this area. Bring in the healing light to protect your intuition and knowing.

- Your energy is getting higher as you sit with self. Visualise your entire energy field clearing from your head to your throat, to your chest, heart, lungs, and into the stomach, into your base, arms, and legs. Your energy field is clearer now, and you are well protected.

- We are all born to have a soft, flexible energy around us. Your energy is flowing more freely through you now. As your energy expands, feel how powerful it is and how it expands out from your body. You can cope with situations. You are getting stronger and stronger.

- You will know, in your awareness, what is real and what is not real, what is yours and not yours. Say to yourself, "I am who I am. I am." It's for you to build the foundation of your structure of who you are and where you need to go.

- Visualise a spotlight as it comes down over you, giving you a sense of space, physically, emotionally, mentally, and spiritually.

- Visualise your energy. Be aware of self and as you look deal with your emotions throughout your life.

- Every breath you take is precious. With every thought you think, you create. For every emotion you feel, let go of what's not yours. As you sit with self, pull in your complete control, trust, belief, and faith within yourself. Allow the white healing energy to become strong around you and throughout you, above and below you and each side of you.

- Feel your body. Don't hold your breath. Breathe in and out gently. Allow the energy to become stronger and stronger in you. Allow the space in front of you to be. Allow your time to be your time. How would you describe yourself? How do you see yourself? How do you listen to yourself? What are you hearing? How do you connect with yourself, with your higher self, your inner voice? Be one with self.

- Allow your eyes to see, allow your ears to hear, allow knowing to happen. Ask your chest to expand and your heart to open up. You have no reason to hide. Just be you sitting with self. Let down all the barriers. You have your protection around you. What do you express for you? What do you really want? Who are you? Let go of all the habits and personalities that don't serve you well. Hold your true personality and create what you want to create in the here and now and for your best future.

- Acknowledge your wisdom and courage. Remember the three centres: your head, heart, and your intuition. Allow your inner voice to come forward and speak your truth. Trust all within.

- Allow the light to shine within you, around you and throughout you, stronger and stronger.

- Accept all of your experiences as you learn to change them into a positive and respect yourself.

- Your energy is heightening now. Bring in your own healing power to heal yourself.

- Allow the white light to turn green. Let this healing light flow to where you need it in your body.

- Bring in all the good experiences from your childhood and your best thoughts about yourself. Acknowledge the good.

Think, "I want to be me." Be who you are. Think, "I am me. Me is who I am." Acknowledge the pain you have experienced through your life, and let it go, correcting muscle and circulation in your body.

- Become aware of your spine as the energy moves up and down, pulling you into the here and now. Visualise pure white light flowing in through your head and throughout your whole body.

- Trust the inner voice. It will always serve you well. Intuition just knows. Feel the power of trust. Allow your trust to become strong and imprint it into your body. Take your control, trust, belief, and faith within yourself. Feel your trust in yourself and in life.

- Be aware of your energy as it settles, now. Become aware of the shift you have made in your energy.

- Your base is your foundation. You need a solid foundation. Bring it in underneath your feet. Stand strong on the learning of your life so far.

- Feel lighter and lighter, clearing off your emotions today of what's not yours.

- Now sit with self.

- Feel yourself grounded as you sit or lie.

- Be one with life, one with you.

- Settle your energy.

- Feel yourself grounded.

- Slowly open your eyes and stretch out your body.

Personalities: Key Points to Remember

- We can look at the various personality traits that we portray and ask ourselves which ones are really us and which are false ones that we created for various reasons and now enter into unconsciously out of habit.

- We have the choice to let go of false personalities and just be ourselves.

- If you don't like yourself, it is actually a distorted image of yourself that you don't like. Your real self, once you see it, is easy for you to love.

Chapter Eleven

Depression

Depression feels like a weight in the body. Old fear-based thoughts and emotions have solidified into a knot that hits the pit of the stomach, causing an imbalance in all the energies of the body. Brain function goes into a disordered state. Hormone levels become imbalanced, sending the body into turbulence. Circulation flows either faster or slower, causing muscle tightness and fatigue. The brain may go into overdrive with obsessive thinking or slow down, giving a numb, foggy feeling. The ability to think clearly is lost. There is a bleak feeling of being stuck in time. There is a feeling of being locked outside of ourselves or trapped deep inside, causing isolation. It can feel like a depth of mental pain has opened up, and we can't get up out of it. Resolving depression is best done piece by piece. It usually cannot be released all at once. Counselling and expressing suppressed feelings and thoughts gives us clarity, releasing ourselves of our depression as we dissolve the knot.

Do not be afraid of life, instead believe life is worth living.

Live life to the full, in the here and now. This belief will help you create your future.

Depression is different for each individual. However, it includes some of the following:

- Feeling low in self.
- Carrying around suppressed emotions which you try to avoid looking at or thoughts you don't want to think.
- Having rushes of overwhelming feelings and thoughts that feel out of control and confusing.
- Feeling like you are falling away from yourself and losing your own identity.
- Having a brain that is in overdrive.
- Devaluing yourself to a low point.
- Feeling like no one understands how you feel, and nobody can help you.
- Feeling depleted and tired with little access to your usual energy.
- Feeling a buzzing sensation in your head or feeling dizzy.
- Feeling agitated in your body, tapping feet, legs hopping, biting nails, excessive fidgeting.
- Suffering from a lot of unexplained aches and pains, especially in the lower back.
- Feeling nauseous and eating more or less than usual.
- Being very withdrawn.
- Feeling extreme loneliness and on the outside of everything.
- Feeling down.
- Feeling trapped in a cycle of thoughts, trapped in your head.
- Carrying around deeply repressed emotions you don't want to remember.
- Feeling like a heavy weight has been placed on you.
- Feeling like everything is wrong.
- Feeling fearful for self and others.
- Thinking self-destructive thoughts.
- Feeling disorientated, without direction in your life.
- Sleeping excessively or having difficulty getting and staying asleep.
- Feeling a pulsating knot in your chest or stomach.
- Heightening sensitivity and negativity caused by nerves in the stomach being overstimulated and

- the muscles of the stomach contracting.
- Feeling an adrenaline rush, being in a constant state of fight or flight.
- Having severe headaches or shooting pain up through the head.
- Being unkind to others, abusive, or violent.
- Feeling overloaded and unable to cope.
- Suffering from diarrhoea or constipation.

If you feel depressed for a period of time, your body crashes as it gets so depleted trying to cope with an unrelenting situation. You feel out of control and unable to cope. You can't breathe properly. There is a lack of oxygen in your whole system. It can feel like there is a tight band around you. You may feel extreme pain, emotionally and physically. You need some help.

Moving Forward with Depression

The smallest step forward in the right direction ends up being the biggest step in your life. Find yourself, be yourself and trust. Take that step.

- Accept you need help and remember that it is ok to need and ask for help. Everyone needs help at some time in their life. Look for it from the people who support you in your life and keep looking until you feel heard, and someone helps you put a plan in place to provide you with what you need to help you cope and feel better. Putting a structure in place for your recovery may include: guidance from a trusted doctor, psychiatrist, or psychologist, counselling; scheduling time and activities with supportive family and friends; learning new ways to soothe yourself, such as tai chi, yoga, breathwork, meditation, listening to music, or watching comedies; or getting involved

- in creative activities such as painting, writing, pottery, design, playing music.

- There are also many organisations that exist to help you, such as Samaritans Ireland. See the resources section for a list of help available.

- Know that you can come through this. Thousands and thousands of people have before you. You are feeling a huge number of past thoughts, feelings, and fears altogether, which is overwhelming. Your strength and power are still there beneath these. You can release all of the pain and find your energy and joy.

- You might need some prescribed medication to get you started on your recovery. If so, accept this as a steppingstone out of despair.

Mental Illness

Sometimes the underlying cause of mental distress is a mental illness such as schizophrenia, bipolar disorders, and severe clinical depression. When a mental illness takes hold, it can feel like you are being locked into a prison of the experience. Thoughts become so big and all-consuming. The small situations of day-to-day life can become insurmountable challenges. In this state, the biggest fear may be that you will never get your mind back. Mental illness can cause severe anxiety, terror, and despair.

If you suffer from mental illness, it's important to confide in someone, a friend, family member or your GP who will listen and hold a supportive space for you to say how you are feeling and to whom you can tell the thoughts that seem to have invaded your mind. Call forth the courage that's in you to be vulnerable and open about what is happening. Accept the help that is there - support organisations, psychiatry, medication, psychotherapy, counselling. Reassure yourself that there are people there to support you through this, that you will be ok, and that balance will come back into your mind.

Sometimes, with the right interventions, the illness is managed for the long term, and other times, there is a cyclical pattern to it, and there are really tough times followed by good times. You can help yourself by watching for early signs that a bad episode is starting and explaining to those close to you when you are well what the slide into these times is like so they can set up the support you need before an episode becomes acute. These signs may include some of the following: not being able to sleep, sleeping around the clock, talking very fast, withdrawing from social interactions, making sudden big plans, being irritable, constant anxiety, engaging in risky behaviour, having obsessive negative thoughts, hallucinations, difficulty concentrating, increasing paranoia, and loss of interest in everyday life. With early intervention, you can get your stability and balance back more quickly with less distress. Be as kind as you can to yourself. Constantly build your self-worth and confidence and give yourself credit for your resilience and courage as you traverse these difficult times.

Will to Live and Suicidal Thoughts

Keeping our will to live strong and focusing on creating a good life for ourselves is especially important for our emotional, mental, and physical well-being. If we give up our will to live, we stop living in the present. Our life-force becomes slow and weakens. A weakening of our will to live can be caused by anxiety, bullying, abuse, shock, trauma, low self-esteem, insecurities, self-destructive thoughts, someone else holding your control, prolonged confusion, regret, false personalities, negativity, resentment, anger, rage, guilt, or fear.

We may start to question our quality of life, thinking thoughts such as:

"What is it all about?"

"I don't care."
"I wish I could close my eyes and not wake up."
"Why is this happening?"
"Nobody understands me."
"Nothing goes right for me."
"I can't get out of bed to face the day."

When we feel sorry for ourselves, negativity heightens. We can experience a feeling of emptiness and isolation.

We might feel as though everyone is putting responsibility on us, that we are just existing. We may feel that there is no hope for us, that nothing is going well, that there is a heavy weight on our chest, that we cannot breathe and are suffocating, and that life is not worth living. We may experience palpitations, panic attacks, mood swings, tiredness, or depression. We may feel locked out of part of ourselves with no access to our coping strategies, stuck in a space outside our body negatively observing ourselves. We find the smallest of tasks very difficult, and we struggle to get through our day.

Thinking and feeling this way for prolonged amounts of time can lead to some people having suicidal thoughts. Sometimes suicidal thoughts may not even belong to the person thinking them. I have seen this many times with clients, particularly young men. Someone close may have died by suicide, and in all of the tormented thinking caused by their death among family and friends, suicidal thoughts can be taken on board by someone who, up to then, may just have been feeling low. Suicidal thoughts diminish a person's life-force, causing them to feel sluggish and heavy. This causes alternating personalities where you feel you are losing control because your thoughts have become delusional. Your fear paralyzes you. All of this puts pressure on your body physically, which can cause terrible physical pain and severe mental distress.

Regaining Your Will to Live

The first step to moving out of this is to acknowledge where you are. You are thinking this way, and it's best to acknowledge that. Denying it to yourself because of your extreme fear, fighting against the thoughts and judging yourself for thinking in such a way adds another layer of mental anguish. Next, know that suicidal thoughts are obsessive, distorted, negative thoughts. You may be in a constant state of terror locked into a small part of yourself, unable to connect with ordinary life going on around you, afraid of what it would mean for you if people knew what you were thinking and how you were feeling. You can, with help, get out of this temporary state. You need to be very brave and tell someone what is going on inside you. Thinking so bleakly is a symptom of depression or mental illness. Know that you actually don't want to die. You just want the pain to end and that there are constructive ways to end the pain and live. You are lost in distressing thoughts. Your biggest fear is taking the risk of looking at your life and expressing what you really feel. You may think that no one will understand. Be brave. Those who love you and professionals who work to help people find their will to live will surprise you by how much they can support you. Be open to receiving their help which may, if necessary, include hospitalisation and medication.

Once you start opening up to people and expressing your pain, the next step is to choose one thing to focus on that would make a positive impact. If you are working, you might, after some time off, cut your work week hours to lessen pressure on yourself. If you are studying, you might drop a subject that doesn't interest you and focus on those that do. Maybe you have a friendship that isn't good for you, and you might make some changes around who you spend time with. If you have started sleeping during the day and staying up all night, you could focus on slowly switching this pattern so that your sleep is more beneficial to you. You could commit to going for a walk every morning. You need to build yourself back up slowly, recover gradually, give yourself time, and nurture yourself with encouragement, rest, good food, counselling, and positive family members and friends.

You will gain strength, courage, and confidence when you stop and look compassionately at yourself in the present. Choose a purpose to help you to step out and move forward. This will give you hope for the future. Then you can come into your own and live your life to the full and let go of the pain. You will be forever proud that you found the resilience in yourself to survive.

A Memorable Writing Experience

My Dad's spirit was very present with us during writing sessions, particularly when we discussed depression and pain, which were states he knew too well. As we'd finish up working on these topics, he would flood the room with love, acknowledgement, pride and strength, giving me the support that he couldn't during his life, reminding me of the bond of love and connection that we share.

A Visualisation to Help You Find Your Hope:

- Sit and take three slow deep breaths.

- Feel the soles of your feet touching the ground.

- In your thoughts, call out to your inner spirit, your higher self.

- Visualise your inner spirit coming forth as a spark of light in the centre of your stomach above your navel.

- Breathe deeply and imagine using your diaphragm as a bellows to help the spark glow and grow into a bright yellow flame of light, your inner spirit.

- Visualise this flame of light brightening more and illuminating your whole stomach and the nerves connected to your stomach.

- Allow this flame of light to soothe you and bring in ease.
- Appreciate the gifts of strength and hope that this brings you in this moment.
- Acknowledge the relief and repeat as needed.

Journal Exercises

Are you stuck in your life with no direction?

Where did this start for you?

Who can you talk to?

What do you need to do or give yourself to change this pattern and habit of thought?

How strong is your life-force?

How strong is your will to live?

Do you question your life, constantly thinking, "I don't want to be here," or "I'm fed up"?

Do you have suicidal thoughts? If so, what has contributed to this?

To whom will you turn to for help?

Make one goal for yourself to move towards.

_____

_____

_____

Depression: Key Points to Remember

- Depression is a tightly wound ball of fear filled negative thoughts, worries, and memories which have become lodged in the body, significantly impeding the natural flow of energy through and around our body.

- Depression causes much distress to our body and mind especially when we feel unable to shift our negative thought patterns or find our coping skills.

- Asking for help and accepting the resulting support helps us to look at and release the causes of depression and recover. *Aware* provides free support by phone, email, and face to face support groups.

- Mental illnesses require long term monitoring and managing. If you suffer with one create a circle of support around yourself which could include family, friends, and professionals. Catch the onset of difficult times so that help can be put in place sooner and the severity and length of these times can be reduced.

- If you have suicidal thoughts know that there is help available to you. Tell someone how you are feeling so that they can put this help into action for you. *Pieta* has a 24hr crisis helpline and provides a free one-to-one counselling service without needing a referral.

- Suicidal thoughts are obsessive negative, distorted thoughts that will dissipate once the experience, thoughts, and feelings that caused them are expressed and compassionately heard.

- Setting small goals and meaningful purposes is a vital part of recovery.

- See the resources section for a comprehensive list of support services available.

Part Three

Building Foundations for a Wonderful Life

Chapter One

How to Value Yourself

We can often judge ourselves harshly and compare ourselves to others in a negative way. When you catch yourself doing this, remind yourself that you are a unique person within yourself. You are equal to all others, not better and not worse. It is your responsibility and duty to yourself to build up your own confidence and self-esteem. We can't expect others to do this for us. We can fall into the trap of looking for our value in the ways others treat us and react to us. This leaves us vulnerable to depend on others to be fair, kind, welcoming, appreciative, and encouraging, which is too much to ask of people.

Our inherent value is within, so we need to stop looking in the wrong place. Are you someone who frequently self-sabotages? Do you constantly question yourself and your ability to cope? Do not look critically at an aspect of yourself and speak hard-heartedly to yourself or about yourself. Soften your words. Everyone is different based on their sensitivity, life experience, personality, interests, and talents. Different and equal.

Don't hide who you really are.

You are the biggest judge of yourself.

Believe in yourself and take back your power.

Look at your sense of worth by asking yourself:
- *Who am **I**?*
- *What is **my** real personality?*
- *What are **my** opinions?*
- *What are **my** hopes for me?*
- *What are **my** dreams for my life?*
- *How do **I** learn? How do **I** take in information? Is it mostly by seeing, by listening, by feeling, or by doing?*

Look at your abilities. Appreciate your strengths and own them. They are unique to you. Look honestly at what you need to improve on and know that you can achieve great things. Value what you need to say. When you are struggling with something, find a safe environment in which to express your difficulty. Ask someone supportive to make some time for you. Then talk openly, clearly expressing what's wrong, without blame. Your clarity, honesty, and courage will lead to new options and solutions.

Decide to be always hopeful and know that the resources to deal with all that comes up in life are there for you. Be yourself in your life. Use your own compass to find your way. Your life is a gift to you and all you meet. Settle into yourself and be true to who you are.

An Exercise to Help Value Yourself More

- Take a few deep, slow breaths. Ground yourself. Bring up a negative thought that you regularly have that makes you feel bad about yourself? Give the part of yourself that thinks such thoughts a name.

- Now sit strongly in your true personality. Bring out the negative personality in front of you. Sit momentarily with it, and your body will tell you how it really feels to be listening to this criticism. Don't shut your feelings down. Acknowledge that this negative talk is not serving you well. What would you say to your named negative personality to empower you to deal with those types of negative thoughts? Play out the conversation in your head. What is the source of this criticism? Sort what's real from what you have added to it. Keep talking to this personality. You can tell this personality that you are giving back to others their part of it -the opinions that don't belong to you, that you can put what's left of this negativity into perspective, that you can take the power you had given to it back. Tell it the learning you have gotten from it and the positive outcome you will turn it into. Tell it what you can work towards to dissolve it completely.

- You need to be very clear with the negative personality. To understand the level of clarity needed, think of a small child who has a burning question. There is something they need to understand, and they will keep asking the question to the adults in their lives until someone gives them a complete and honest answer. When they are satisfied, the issue is dropped, and their focus is free to move on. Just like the child who needs an answer, your negative personality has an issue that it will not drop until you deal with it clearly and honestly. Feel it! Open the personality out for you to look at its composition and source and deal with it, and then it will dissipate.

- Place your hand on where this negativity had affected you, such as your heart, head or stomach and flow healing energy into your body, filling the space with love and compassion.

- Say positive things to yourself and relish the feeling that this brings into your body.

- Visualise the path to your goals lighting up as you regularly think empowering thoughts. From time to time, that negative personality can reappear, but if it does, you will be able to sit more comfortably with it and know that you have dealt with it and can send it on its way and out of your head.

> *Journal Exercises*
>
> *Who are you?*
>
> *Do you respect yourself?*
>
> *Does your inner voice generally speak positively or negatively?*
>
> *What are your values?*
>
> *How is your self-worth and self-confidence?*
>
> *What are your hopes and dreams for yourself?*
>
> *What are your strengths and talents?*

Stepping Back - Valuing Yourself

I was in my late thirties before I learned to value myself truly. Up to that point in my life, I believed other people when they told me my value was being quiet, accommodating, and unassertive. I worked hard to fulfil responsibilities and roles put upon me to reassure myself that I had value. The breakthrough for me occurred when I took ownership of myself and started to live from the new belief that I owned myself.

Owning myself gave me back my power. I decided to accept myself, to love myself unconditionally. I accepted my faults but took the firm position that I would no longer engage in self-sabotaging thoughts. I stepped into owning my gifts. I knew I was a good listener and focused on that unique gift of seeing the full truth behind any situation. I am honest and kind. I am good at giving people acknowledgement, clarity, advice, and encouragement. I committed to living the rest of my life in a way that valued, developed, and shared these gifts, and I haven't looked back.

Honesty

Being honest is checking in with yourself and being true to yourself. Sometimes we like to alter the truth to a self-serving half-truth when we feel uncomfortable about something. We can twist things and exaggerate aspects. We make up lies to make our stories fit a situation for our own purpose.

I am the person I am today through facing life's challenges.

I am who I am, and I don't need to explain myself to anyone, only myself.

Why Are We Dishonest?

- We can get off the hook for something we did that we don't want to take responsibility for.
- We get lots of attention for having the "best" or "worst" story.
- We can get support for our position in a disagreement.
- We use lies to change our position from feeling inferior to feeling superior.

What Do We Lose When We Lie?

- We worry about the truth coming out.

- We cause unnecessary hurt to others by gossiping, spreading rumours, criticising, and making judgements.

- We know the attention that our lie gets us is not based on the truth and, therefore, is not beneficial to us.

- We cause ourselves confusion about what is real. We can start believing that our lies are true.

- We conform to friendships that do not fit with us.

- We feel disconnected and lonely because we made up a story to fit in with others, and we know we are not our true selves.

- We feel weak. We have diminished our power by giving our attention to what we know is not true.

- We damage our self-confidence and self-worth.

There is great power in taking responsibility for your own words and your own actions. Be present in your own self. See yourself and others clearly. Then speak and act the truth.

> *Journal Exercises*
>
> *How honest are you with yourself?*
>
> *Do you live your life true to yourself or do you pretend?*
>
> *Do you frequently exaggerate?*
>
> *How confident are you with being honest?*
>
> *Do you feel worthy of your truth?*

The Mirror

Everyone in my life has something to teach me. There is a purpose in my learning in accepting the positive and letting go of the negative.

Every relationship we have and everyone we meet in our day act as a mirror for us. Every interaction with another shows us things about ourselves. We then decide if it is something we want to develop and build on or something we want to let go of. When we notice ourselves admiring another person's character, we discover the qualities in ourselves that are important to us, such as kindness, loyalty, gentleness, an adventurous spirit, persistence, optimism, fairness, integrity, and a sense of fun. When we witness others living their life's purpose, it can inspire us to live ours. When we see the vulnerability in others, it can help us accept and heal the vulnerable parts of ourselves. When someone irritates, annoys, or lets us down, the situation can show us something in ourselves that needs to be addressed. Instead of just jumping into blaming and criticising, we can stand back from the situation for a few moments.

Ask yourself these questions:
- What is it about them that is annoying me so much?
- What are they doing that is causing me to be upset or angry?
- What does their behaviour trigger in me?
- Does what they are doing affect me because it reminds me of a previous upsetting experience in my life?
- Am I upset and annoyed because their behaviour is actually mirroring an aspect of myself that I don't like?
- What do I see as I look in the mirror?
- Is the annoyance a signpost that indicates something I need to develop in myself?

- What is their behaviour showing me about myself?

Imagine yourself as a lion. You were a young lion cub, and now you are growing into an adult lion. As a cub, you had a lot of insecurity, but now, as you grow, you are gathering the strengths of bravery, wisdom, knowledge, dignity, self-respect, and strength. When someone annoys you look into the mirror and see what aspect of you needs to grow. What old behaviour and ways of thinking have you outgrown that you need to shed? What quality do you need to give to yourself to help you cope and flourish? Acknowledge the learning that every life experience brings to you.

As well as everyone acting as a mirror for you, you also act as a mirror to yourself. Is the 'you' that goes about your day interacting with others a true reflection of your real self? Does your personality and personal style express who you really are? When you look in your mirror, are you going in a direction in your life that really resonates with you? Are there changes you would like to make? Put things in place for yourself so your future reflects your real passions, interests, values, and goals.

> *Journal Exercises*
>
> *Think of someone you admire. Which qualities and strengths do you also have that you could pay more attention to and further develop?*
>
> *Think of someone who annoys you. Are they mirroring something in you that you need to look at and resolve?*
>
> *What aspect of your personality do you not like being shown to you?*
>
> *Does your day-to-day life mirror the qualities of who you really are?*

Comparing Ourselves to Others

A certain amount of comparison is beneficial. It helps us look around at the variety in the world and choose our likes and dislikes. We choose the things that fit or resonate with who we are and the things that don't. Comparing helps us to find our identity and choose what we want in our lives.

However, sometimes we compare ourselves to others because:

- We want to be the best or feel that we are better than someone else.

- We want to be someone that others will follow in an ego-driven way.

- We want to fit in at any cost to ourselves as we don't want to be teased or feel inferior.

We may compare our clothes, weight, height, hair, looks, talents, cleverness, family, wealth, houses, cars, religion, skin colour, food likes, birthday parties, photos on social media, phone brands, presents, holidays, exam results, school projects, knowledge of film or music, knowledge of trends, numbers of friends, game consoles, and so much more.

When we compare ourselves to others, we can put ourselves under too much pressure. We then feel stressed and vulnerable. We give away our confidence in ourselves. We lose our identity taking on an identity that is an imagined combination of other peoples' identities. We give away our power and feel anxious and angry. This is too high of a price to pay. It is a betrayal of yourself to try to change yourself into someone you are not. Sometimes we have the illusion that we need to be like others or own certain things to be happy when we are actually betraying what is really important to us in order to fit in.

When you compare yourself to others and say unkind things to yourself, notice this impact on you physically, mentally, and emotionally. Stop comparing! Believe in yourself and the person you are. Stay true to your own values to what you think and see as important. What do you value the most? Relationships, family, friendship, kindness, fun, education, honesty, achievement, dignity, hard work, common sense, optimism, being wealthy, respect, creativity, support, thoughtfulness, decisiveness, loyalty, tolerance, persistence, trust, being cool, being fashionable, intelligence, good humour, insightfulness, etc.

Be kind to yourself and value your uniqueness. We are all different. We all have our own gifts, paths, and creative ways to be in the world. Be assertive. Let go of judging others. Focus on being clear about who you are and where you need to go in your life.

We cannot judge other people because we do not understand what their life is about. By understanding yourself without judgement, you will have compassion for others.

> ***Journal Exercises***
>
> *Who do you compare yourself to?*
>
> *Do you judge yourself and others?*
>
> *What lengths do you go to, to fit in?*
>
> *Do you value your own uniqueness?*

Connecting Your Logic, Emotions, and Intuition

Having confidence in your ability to make good decisions for yourself adds to your sense of self-worth. When we have a decision to make, a worry to sort, or a situation that needs our judgement, we often rely on our logical mind to work things out. We can get a bit lost in our own thoughts and others' opinions, leading to confusion and indecision.

A useful process to practise is to organise three centres of your body to work together: your brain, your heart, and your gut. Each of these centres has a unique intelligence. When we allow the logic of our brain, the emotions of our heart, and the intuition of our gut to link up, we see things clearly. You can allow communication to flow between each centre. Following the steps below will give you clarity and help you move forward in a true way to your identity.

- Take back your control, trust, belief, and faith within yourself. Take ownership of your identity and your own strength. Acknowledge your first sense of the situation. Depending on your personality, it may be lots of thought, an emotional feeling, or a sense of knowing in your gut.

- Start processing the situation with your brain, the centre of logic, information, and creative thinking. Pause and look at your thoughts. What do you think about the person, situation or worry? Pull out what needs to be cleared from the situation, such as others' opinions and your own worries. Often our worries are triggered by how this situation mirrors something that upset us in the past, and these worries do not actually belong to the present.

- Visualise a bin beside you and drop all your worries and negative thoughts into it.

- Bring in positive thoughts to the situation.

- Instead of analysing and judging your thoughts, bring them down through your brain, connecting the thoughts with your heart.

- Check-in with your heart. Open your heart to the situation. How do you feel about it? Name your feelings. Stay with this for a few moments. Acknowledge what you are feeling.

- Now that you have checked in with your heart, bring this situation down into your stomach and gut into your intuition. What is your gut sense in relation to this situation? Acknowledge the knowing that you sense in your gut. Go with your first realisation. Trust it.

- Allow a synergy of information from the three centres to occur and reveal your knowing of the truth of the situation.

- Take ownership of your decision or truth in relation to the situation. Allow your actions to flow from this clarity.

Frequent use of this method will help you make good decisions for yourself and help you see tricky situations clearly so that you can move through your day-to-day life in a much more confident way.

> ### *Journal Exercises*
>
> *When you have a decision to make, do you tend to look at the situation mostly logically, emotionally, or intuitively?*
>
> *Can you clearly see a situation, or do you tend to look at it just from one viewpoint?*
>
> *How does looking at situations connecting the information from your logical mind, your emotional heart, and your intuitive gut change your perspective?*

Stepping Back - Listening to My Gut

I have always had extraordinarily strong intuition. In my childhood, I couldn't cope with the overwhelming emotions that accompanied what I intuitively observed in people in my everyday life. I tried to block my emotions and instead deal with things only with logical thinking in my head. This wasn't the best course of action as it numbed my ability to feel, which led to a lot of physical pain and panic attacks.

When I started to look honestly at myself in my thirties, all of this stored emotion began to unravel and be released. During this period, I had a tough time health-wise with a constantly upset stomach. I trusted that by going through this, things were going to get better for me. I started to trust my intuition more and allowed my stomach and heart to open. I started to soften and feel my true emotions in the present moment. Sometimes emotions rushed into my body and then I would have to look at what I was feeling. I brought in my logic to understand the feeling and then connected with my intuition. With trust and practice, clarity and a sense of flow came into my life.

How to Value Yourself: Key Points to Remember

- We value ourselves when we stop critically comparing ourselves to others and instead look inside and decide to develop the gifts we find.

- We can learn to talk back to negative beliefs we carry about ourselves and dissipate the negativity.

- Honesty allows us to feel that we are good enough.

- Everyone around us acts as a mirror for us highlighting both our qualities and weaknesses. We can be open to the constructive insights that they give us.

- We can let go of the pressure of judging ourselves and others in a harsh way when we take an honest look at the reason for our comparison.

- We can make good decisions when we allow the relevant information to flow through our mind, heart, and gut connecting our logic, emotions, and intuition.

Chapter Two

Friendships and Relationships

You get the best out of other people when you give the best of yourself.

Friends have a mutual bond and enjoy spending time together. They interact with ease, with a flow of chat and ideas. Friends support each other and encourage each other to follow their interests and goals. Good friends respect each other's values and boundaries. They do not ask each other to change who they are. Within a good friendship, you can speak freely. Ideally, friends do not hurt each other, and if they mess up, they apologise, and they forgive each other. Sometimes friends clash due to one person seeking control, differing opinions, interference from others, parents, siblings or other friends, competitiveness, changing interests, or jealousy. Observe how you feel after spending time with a friend. Are you buzzing, content, or feeling drained and tired? This will give you insight into the type of friendship you have and how the friendship is currently impacting you.

Things don't always go smoothly with friends, but the support, sense of belonging, and fun that friends bring into your life make friendships very worthwhile. Through your friendships, you develop your personality, interests, knowledge base, opinions, values, empathy, ability to resolve conflict, sense of humour, personal boundaries, likes and dislikes, communication skills, sense of fun, and resilience. Every friendship is unique, and within it, you exchange a particular set of qualities. Friendship allows you the privilege of pointing out to others what is wonderful about them.

When choosing friends, you sometimes need to choose between having a certain image and being happy. Do you veer towards the popular person and try to fit into being someone they would want to be friends with, or do you choose someone that fits you? The person who fits you has similar values. Which of these values below stand out as being particularly important to you? Enthusiasm, achievement, cheerfulness, adventure, creativity, fame, dependability, order, peace, effectiveness, health and fitness, truth, helping others, privacy, respect, honesty, independence, common sense, closeness, integrity, knowledge, justice, leadership, cooperation, sportsmanship, loyalty, personal development, or wisdom. Know who you are and choose your friends accordingly.

Some people find it easy to make friends, and some find it more difficult. If you find it difficult, ask yourself if you have opted out of seeking friendship, learning to live mostly in your own space and finding it hard to let people in. Did this difficulty start due to conflict with a parent, sibling, or friend? The key to finding a good friend is first to develop a friendship with yourself.

Working on Our Relationship with Ourselves First

Take some time to work on your relationship with yourself so that you can understand and find the value and connection in your relationships and friendships with others.

To do this:
- Close your eyes. Imagine a mirror in front of you and see your reflection looking back at you.

- Say hello to yourself. Allow a connection to flow heart to heart. Are you friends with yourself? Listen to your answer. Decide to develop your friendship with yourself.

- Imagine chatting with yourself about your likes and dislikes, your values and beliefs, your hopes and dreams, struggles and fears, and your relationship with yourself. Get to know your own strengths and qualities, and values.

- Speak kindly to yourself. Build up a strong foundation of who you are. What do you need to give to you? Is it kindness, support, encouragement, decisiveness, or a goal? Is it control, trust, belief, or faith? Is it nourishing food, more sleep, time outdoors, or time doing things you love?

- Repeat this exercise until you get comfortable with and accept who you are. If you find it difficult to get to this point, consider doing a few counselling sessions to find your blocks and release unhelpful thoughts about yourself.

When you are a good friend to yourself, you will not feel needy. You are ready to make good friendships as you are strong and ready to choose who you would like as a friend. Get involved in activities that you enjoy and be open to making friends. A huge number of friends is not necessary, but one or two good friends add support, fun, companionship, and learning to our lives.

As we move into and through our life stages, our opinions and identity alter and change. We can find that close friendships don't fit us anymore. You may have had a friend since you were young, and things no longer feel right between you. One or both of your identities has changed. Your likes, interests, and values are out of kilter. When you have been remarkably close to someone, and then you are not spending time together anymore, you can feel a huge sense of loss, like you have lost part of your identity. It can feel as though part of you has separated. We have to learn to accept that friendships can end or become less close. We can focus on the wonderful experiences, learning, and fun that we have gained from these relationships and mentally and emotionally take ownership of these treasures. We can spend time affirming ourselves using the mirror image exercise to build ourselves up again and be open to making new friendships.

> *Journal Exercises*
>
> *Are you a good friend to yourself?*
>
> *Are you a loyal and honest friend to others?*
>
> *What sort of friends do you have?*
>
> *Do you and your friends fit well together as a friendship group?*
>
> *What role do you take in your friendship group? Are you a leader, a minder, a pleaser, a drama queen, a shy person, etc.?*
>
> *What do you need to do to be true to who you are when you are with your friends?*

Relationships

Within a good relationship, we create a great friendship, experience reciprocated love and support, and are emboldened into being our best selves. We make a connection with each other and form a strong bond.

Possible relationships begin with an attraction to someone, and a rush of emotions comes in. We want to spend time with this person, and if the attraction is reciprocated, we may choose to start a relationship and strengthen the connection. We get to know the other person better and learn about each other's personality, interests, opinions, wants, needs, and goals. It is a really exciting time!

Understanding the Roadblocks to a Fulfilling, Happy Relationship

- It is often the case that we are attracted to a person whose personality is the opposite of us in some ways. Our partner's personality and opinions can be stronger or softer than ours. If this is the case, it is important for us to be conscious of not controlling one another. We can stay true to ourselves and our own likes and dislikes. We can acknowledge that we'll think differently about some things. Respect and having boundaries are essential in a good relationship.

- If we change ourselves a lot to fit in with our partner when we get into a relationship, we will find this false personality more and more difficult to maintain as time goes on. After a few months, our partner will begin to feel that we are not the person they started going out with, and they would be correct because that person doesn't actually exist. A habit of morphing ourselves into a false personality is caused by insecurity. The pretence is not going to lead to happiness. The relationship will not be a good one if you are not true to yourself and honest with your partner.

- We may find that after some time in a relationship, a side of our partner emerges that was initially hidden from us. This can happen suddenly or gradually. We need to trust our gut feelings and act when we know we need to get out of the relationship. Signs include a partner that scares you, is overly critical of you, is nasty during disagreements, tries to control you, tries to manipulate you, or tries to isolate you from your family or friends.

- It is easy to slip into learned habits in relationships that we have picked up from our parents and the relationships we have grown up with. Many of these may be good and worth modelling. However, if one of your parents was controlling, jealous, angry, manipulative, or insecure, be mindful that these characteristics are not brought into your relationship. Let go of any habit that does not reflect love, trust, and respect for one another. Build up your own strengths, self-belief, and set of values upon which you build your relationship.

- Sometimes family or friends can interfere in our relationships, pushing forth their opinion of our partner. They may see a trait in the other person which you need to be aware of. Trust your gut to see if their opinions are fair or are coming from jealousy or prejudice. Then detach from the surrounding drama, be clear about how you read the whole situation and follow your truth.

- In our late teens and twenties, we may see being in a relationship as a ticket to adulthood. Starting a relationship does not make us a fully-fledged adult. Creating a good relationship based on love, boundaries, trust, and respect is a wonderful life experience and develops maturity, but that maturity is not an instant thing.

- We may have a tendency to isolate ourselves from our friends once we are in a relationship focusing all our attention on our partner. We may lose ourselves in the relationship and exclude our friends. This is not a good move long-term. It's important to keep a supportive group of friends. New relationships are exciting but need to have their place timewise. To keep our lives balanced, enjoy maintaining friendships and continue to spend time on your interests and leisure activities.

- When in a relationship, we may feel pressure either from ourselves or our partner to look a certain way, maintain a certain image involving expensive and time-consuming treatments, and have a particular dress style or a certain physique. Sometimes we can go too far and lose sight of our real selves in the mirror. Check in with yourself about what feels comfortable and reflects the real you when you choose clothes, a hairstyle, makeup, etc. You needn't let yourself be pressured into having to look a certain way. Instead, honour yourself and your body.

- Sometimes we may have difficulty accepting and being confident in our sexuality or gender identity. Honour your sexuality, being gay, heterosexual, bisexual, etc. Know what you want and need, and do not allow yourself to be pushed towards doing something that you do not feel comfortable with. Be open and honest with your partner and enjoy your sexuality.

- Sometimes we may not feel supported by our partner. The foundation of a good relationship is support. Throughout your life, when you are in a relationship, ask yourself, "Do I feel supported? Do I support my partner? Do we help each other through unexpected challenges such as illness, an unplanned pregnancy, grief, job loss or upset? Do we support each other's purpose, goals, and dreams? Are we able to express our love for each other and how we feel in a true manner in a way that suits us?" We need to communicate clearly the support we need, reassuring words, help with the house or children, encouragement to follow our dreams, quality time together, thoughtfulness etc., and build good levels of support into our relationships.

- We may not be able to manage arguments well within a relationship. When disagreements occur, express what you need to say as calmly and respectfully as you can. Listen to your partner and what they are really saying. Disagreements can clear the air and allow your need for support, an apology, acknowledgement, or reassurance to be expressed. Resolving disagreements is about understanding each other's morals, values, and vulnerabilities. It's important to communicate honestly and choose a time to sit with each other to talk openly.

- Sometimes our relationships end, and we need to take care of ourselves as we recover. If your relationship ends, take the good from it, own it and bring that with you into future experiences. Get support from friends and family if you have difficulty letting go and give yourself time to heal and feel strong in yourself and process the relationship before starting a new one.

Through your shared life experiences and trusted connection, long-term relationships can create a deep friendship, unconditional love, a great understanding of one another, and a wider foundation that adds to our strength and courage as we pursue our life purpose and goals.

Journal Exercises

Are you friends with yourself? Are you being your own person in your life?

Are you or will you be true to yourself in relationships, true to your interests, your personality, your likes, and dislikes?

Do you see your friendships as important when you are going out with someone as when you are not?

How much are you influenced by others' gossip and drama when you are going out with someone or are attracted to someone?

Which roadblocks affect you in your relationship?

What can you do to bring more fulfilment and happiness into your relationship?

Friendships and Relationships: Key Points to Remember

- Being a good friend to yourself sets you up for welcoming good friendships and relationships into your life.

- Good relationships are built on respect, healthy boundaries, staying true to our real selves, a sense of safety, reflecting on our habits, trusting our gut feelings, maturity, honouring our body and sexuality, receiving, and giving support, and respectful and honest communication.

- When a relationship ends you can take the good from it and own it as part of yourself and then process and release the aspects of it that were not as you would have liked.

Chapter Three

Learning

Your ability to learn is far beyond what you currently imagine. There are four main styles of learning. As you read about them, you will realise the ones you naturally use. With this clarity, you can learn how to develop these styles further to boost your learning power. It is very worthwhile to think about incorporating the other learning styles as they suit different subjects.

The foundation for all learning styles is presence, to be actually in your body. Without presence, we do not have the ability to focus, so we cannot take information in effectively. Lack of focus often starts at a young age and is caused by disassociating yourself from the present moment. When there is something in the present that we do not want to hear, see, or feel, we often remove our attention from the present moment. What distracts you? Is it noise, others' emotions, dynamics between family, friends, workmates, classmates, movement, or colours in your field of vision, or your own thoughts? When your attention leaves the present, ask yourself, "Where are my thoughts? Are my thoughts racing, jumping from topic to topic? Is my attention in the past or the future? Am I aware of my body, or have I disconnected from the present and floated off into a daydream? What am I gaining by leaving 'the here and now'?"

To learn, you need to bring yourself back to the present moment. Bring your attention fully into your own body. Take a couple of deep breaths. Sit into your own space in the room. Visualise a connection between your feet and the ground. Imagine a flow of energy coming from the ground up through your body. If you have any doubts about your learning ability, take a few moments to clear your hang-ups. Mentally give back criticism that others have shared with you and reason with your negative self-talk. Breathe out any self-sabotaging thoughts and release the accompanying feelings replacing them with the energy of inspiration, enthusiasm, and possibility. Trust in your ability to learn information more easily and faster than ever before as you find your best way to learn.

Next, imagine being surrounded by four pillars of beautiful white light to protect you in your own space. Visualise a filing cabinet that holds files, each labelled with the name of one of the topics or subjects you are studying. When you are starting a class or a study session, visualise opening the relevant file so that you can put the new stream or chunk of information in it and remember to close the file again after the learning, so your brain doesn't have to deal with being overloaded with lots of different topics being open at once.

You are now ready to be open and engage with the information being presented and what works best for you to bring your learning to life. You can use the following learning styles to take in the information. Play with these styles and see how your learning ability and speed can increase.

The Four Learning Styles

1. Visual Learning - Learning by Seeing

Visual learning involves looking carefully at what we are learning and bringing the information into our brain as pictures and videos. To use visual memory, own your space 360 degrees around you. Visualise images and film of the information you are learning in the space at arm's length out in front of you. Take your time to work on the images so that they contain the meaning and the important details of what you need to take in. Use colour, originality, and humour in your images to highlight important points and make them memorable. Practise letting the images go and recalling them a few times to consolidate them. When they feel good to you, imagine yourself filing them as visual files, for future reference, in your long-term memory filing cabinet.

2. Emotional Learning - Learning by Feeling

Emotional learning involves tuning into the feelings in our bodies that the information we are learning brings up. The information can then be stored with the feeling as a file and can be recalled when needed. This can help with studying novels and plays as we imagine the characters' feelings throughout a story, and the details of the story can be connected to our feelings. We could use it to learn historical facts by imagining how it felt to have lived through various events and times.

We can consolidate our learning by discussing the emotions that come up as we are learning particular things. We can check our answers in tests by sensing with our gut if our answers feel right, and if they don't, ask ourselves what we need to add to correct them. We can organise our information into lines in order to remember it and tune into what the information feels like as a stream of thought in our head. Try this out and incorporate the other learning styles into your stream of information, such as tuning into the feeling of a stream of images of what we are learning.

3. Auditory Learning - Learning by Listening

Auditory learning involves listening carefully to words as we learn. We are present in our body and engage with the words being spoken or read and focus on understanding what we are hearing. We then store the information as files of meaning. Dialogical learning, where we engage in an open group discussion about the information we are learning, helps us add to what we know about a topic and develop further understanding. People who are naturally good at learning by listening, notice sounds, sound volume and quality, and enjoy listening to radio shows, podcasts, etc. If you want to develop your ability to use this learning style, work on being very present in your body as you listen and ask questions to help you to fully understand what is being taught. Notice the environment in which you like to study. Do you like quiet in the background or to learn with music at a certain volume in the background?

4. Kinaesthetic Learning - Learning by Doing
Kinaesthetic learning is learning by doing something physical. We involve our sense of touch and physical movement in our learning, leaving an imprint of the action in our body. We physically act out the learning, step by step, and practise the information bringing it through the body. We learn kinaesthetically outside, connected to nature. It involves using materials to learn, like how we learned to add when we started school using counters. We use learning by doing to learn the important practical skills of life, such as organising our belongings, keeping our home clean, cooking, and doing laundry, or learning to drive. We use it to develop particular skills such as playing a musical instrument, typing, doing surgery, operating a crane, dancing. We can also use it to learn information by writing keywords a few times using big writing while feeling the pressure and direction of the pencil or by experimenting and being involved in projects. Developing your learning by doing is all about being prepared to have a go.

Make today a learning day, learning new skills and acknowledging what you have learned. It will boost your confidence.

Exercise to Help with Anxiety During Exams

When you are getting ready to sit your exam and waiting for your exam paper, take a few moments to familiarise yourself with your surroundings. Create your own space by visualising a bubble of protection around you, the edge of which is at arm's length, 360 degrees around you. Be in the present time, here and now. Be aware of your whole body, from your head down to your feet. Visualise white light down through the body, anchoring you into the ground. Take a couple of moments and feel your grounding.

Don't take too seriously the concerns and worries of your fellow students, as this will only heighten your own worries and anxieties. Let go of other people's worries and clear your head space. Take a few moments to sit with yourself and look at the pressure and worries within. Breathe in and out gently. Take a deep breath. Hold to the count of three. Release it, clearing your head, chest, and stomach. Repeat this breath work three times.

- Name the foremost negative thought you are giving attention to, changing it to the best possible, positive outcome for you.

- Acknowledge any tightness in your chest in a calm and caring way with yourself. As the heart races, give it care and calm by breathing more slowly and deeply.

- Acknowledge the sensations in your stomach, naming the feeling or thought. Let it be. "I'm upset, nervous. I don't know what to expect! Will I do well?"

- Acknowledge that all you can do at that moment is the best you can and keep breathing gently.

- Remember that all you have studied and the information you have learned are stored in your memory and brain. Trust what you've heard in class is also stored if you haven't studied as much as you might like to have. Visualise your mind like a filing cabinet. Pull out the subject that is relevant. Concentrate only on that. Bring the information up and imagine it, arranged, on a whiteboard, out in front of your mind's eye.

- When you are sitting with your exam paper in front of you, scan the questions and if you have the option to select questions, choose the topics you are most comfortable with. Then do not rush the brain by thinking about all the questions before you start. If you do this, you will probably feel confused because you are looking at some tough questions, and panic might set in, causing the brain's memory to freeze. Instead, trust that the relevant information will come to you for each answer as you focus on the questions, one at a time.

- If you can't remember information and feel panic during an exam, you will be ok. It's caused by a large rush of thoughts that overwhelm the brain giving you a blank feeling. Instead of panicking, understand that your brain needs a moment. Stop trying to think of answers for a minute. Instead, focus on your breath. Feel yourself reconnecting with your body. Breathe calmly and slowly. Lots of oxygen will be available for your brain. Allow your mind to clear and your heart to relax. Give yourself a couple of moments to settle.

- Then continue your paper by looking at the question and answering it to the best of your ability in the allocated time. Once it's finished, move on to the next question and so on. If you get blank or feel unsure about a question, don't focus too hard. Instead, move on to the next question. You can always come back to that question later and answer it to the best of your ability.

- Once you have finished, do a quick reread of all your answers, checking through each one.

- Make sure you breathe gently, clearing your head, throat, chest, and stomach as you work.

- When the exam is over, don't self-sabotage by analysing the questions with your peers. Instead, trust that you have done your best and that all will be well.

Feel your body present in the here and now and feel grounded.

> *Journal Exercises*
>
> *What do you need to do to help you focus and concentrate?*
>
> *Which learning style(s) comes naturally to you?*
>
> *Which learning style(s) could you develop?*
>
> *Which subjects suit you?*

Stepping Back - Uncovering How We Learn

Challenges are opportunities for your growth.
You can handle any situation that comes your way.
Trust and believe in yourself.

I struggled with literacy learning in school. I have dyslexia, but this was not diagnosed at the time. Reading took huge effort as recognising certain letters and their sequence was difficult at the pace required for fluent reading.

Over time, my reading improved, but I was still spelling many words as they were pronounced as a young adult. I was very organised in work and created strategies that helped me overcome and hide my difficulties. For example, I often wrote tricky words quickly in pencil and then wrote them properly later when I had a chance to check the dictionary. Yet, while I mastered functional literacy through sheer persistence, I have always been very quick to learn practical tasks. Once someone shows me how to do something once, I have it. I also have the gift of my intuition which helps me read a situation clearly and know what information is important to remember. I have accepted my learning style and have developed strategies so that I can relax and enjoy learning.

Learning: Key Points to Remember

- To learn you first need to be present in your body.
- We can visualise our learning and store it as images and video.
- We can store information by connecting it to the feeling it gives us when we focus on it.
- By being present and focused on our listening we can extract key concepts from what we hear and store the information as files of meaning.
- Kinaesthetic learning involves bringing learning through the body and acting out the information so we can remember it.
- If you have an exam coming up remember to try out the exercise given to help to lessen your anxiety.

Chapter Four

Your Time

We understand time as the twenty-four-hour clock and as the past, present, and future. However, I want to show you a new concept about time: *Your Time*. We all have our own time, our own ideal rhythm, pace, and power of presence for moving through the day.

Look at your day. Do you allow yourself the time you need to get ready in the morning, or are you rushing around the house at the last minute, feeling incredibly stressed? Do you feel present as you move through the day, hearing and seeing what is going on around you, taking in information, dealing well with your emotions or do you feel confused, inattentive, moody, forgetful, negative, and worried?

When we feel rushed and overwhelmed, we are out of our own time. We can stop for a minute and look at where our thoughts are.

Are you:

- Thinking about upsetting past events and emotional baggage which heightens your anxiety? The past is gone, and time has changed. Those thoughts do not belong in the present, so they do not fit. Your attention has gone back into the past, taking much of your power to deal with the present.

- Thinking about the future, busily planning, or worrying about future events, analysing every detail, imagining every possible scenario? Your attention gets stuck in an imagined future made of a loop of turbulent thoughts. You are not in your time. While it is good to set your purpose and goals, you need to trust that all will unfold. The future has not happened yet, so come back to your present time.

- Flitting about in distracting activities, losing time on your phone, or playing video games to avoid feeling the emotions that arise for being in your past or future?

- Fitting in with other peoples' time? Are you in your family's time? Are you in your friend's time? Are you feeling pressure to be spending your time doing what others think you should be doing? If you live in their time, you are not being present or living in your own time.

Wherever our attention has gone, we can call ourselves back into our body. We can gather our thoughts and come back to the present. In our own time, our day is peaceful rather than rushed. Things flow along. We can put structure on our day and assign enough time to do the things we need to do. We can make time to solve or let go of things that are bothering us. In our own time, we feel confident that we can continuously manage the present, so there is no need for worry. We feel content and happy in ourselves.

You may have to live a good amount of your day in the rhythm of family life and also in the rhythm of our school or workday. Put structure on your day to the best of your ability but be flexible with changes that you may have to make. It is important for you to live in your own time too. You can do this by giving yourself an amount of time each day, even small amounts of time, to check in with yourself and see how you are doing, have a cup of tea or do whatever you enjoy just for yourself. For example, spend ten minutes listening to music, meditating, dancing, drawing, gardening, exercising, walking, baking, designing, or playing with a pet. If you have a bit longer, you could make something, bake, write in a journal, read a good book, watch a funny programme, or chat with someone uplifting.

Choose something that helps you to feel comfortable in your own space. This will give you a feeling of being in your own time and bring this quality of being into your day. You will feel the power of your presence. The first exercise in part four is the grounding practice, a very effective tool to bring you into your own time.

Relax, enjoy the journey of your life. There is no need to rush through life, stop and be present.

Making Time for Fun

Experiencing fun is feeling a rush of happiness. It is a rising feeling and an outburst of joy, lightness, excitement, achievement, or creativity. It involves laughter, enjoying the moment and having no expectations of a particular outcome. Following our own interests brings fun into our lives. Fun comes from things that we choose to do ourselves, without pressure from others. We can bring more fun into our lives by incorporating time with people we love and a little spontaneity.

> **Journal Exercises**
>
> *Where are you in time? Where are your thoughts in time? Is most of your attention spent in the past, present, or future?*
>
> *Do you rush time constantly leaving things to the last moment such as getting ready to leave the house, making decisions, or completing projects?*
>
> *Do you live in your time or someone else's time? Are you respecting your own rhythm or living at the pace of someone else's expectations?*
>
> *Do you frequently flow in your time, where your thoughts are fully in the present and you get immersed in what you are doing?*

Stepping Back - Honouring My Time

During my marriage, I felt like I was always running against the clock. I rushed through each day, trying to fulfil all my responsibilities. I took on more than I could fit into a day, constantly feeling under pressure and often running late. I had a profound realisation one day after my marriage ended. I was delayed in town and rang my sister to say that I would be back at the house later than I had intended. She quickly told me that I wasn't answerable to her for what I did at any time of the day. Her well-meaning and truthful comment took me by surprise as I realised I constantly accounted for my time to other people.

In that instant, I freed myself from running to other people's time and took ownership of my own time. Each new day is filled with opportunities. I balanced my time each day between a reasonable amount of work, time with my sons, fulfilling responsibilities that I choose to take on, and time for me which includes things I enjoy such as going on a walk, taking a nap, relaxing with TV, or spending time with loved ones.

I find the process of grounding myself a great way to start a potentially busy day.

Instead of rushing and suddenly feeling overwhelmed, as was frequently my old way of being, I take a few moments to calm and ground myself. I reason with myself that there is no benefit to racing through the day with my mind flooded with everything I have to do. I take a deep breath and ask myself what I need to do first. I allow my day to flow accordingly with my work. I stay present in each task giving it my full attention to completion before moving on to the next thing. If something happens to interrupt my day, I deal with it as it presents itself. I remember that some things can be attended to later in the week.

Your Time: Key Points to Remember

- To live in your own time, your own rhythm, is to live in a state of peace.

- When you are in your own time you are not torturing yourself with replays of the past or imagined futures. You are powerfully present.

- Small amounts of time that we gift to ourselves can really change the quality of our day, even if we have a lot of responsibilities.

Chapter Five

The Amazing Gift of Life

You have been given the great honour of living a life on earth. You now have the choice and power to live it as you wish. Your power to create and achieve is far beyond what you imagine. If you have someone who sees the real you and believes in you, it is easier to see and experience this. If you have had a tough start in life with little support, you just need to focus a bit harder to believe in yourself. Once you work on gaining your control, trust, belief, and faith within yourself, life will start unfolding for you in amazing ways. You will create your hopes and dreams. Look forward. The high points in your life are still to come. Remember, you are born pure and able to help yourself and create the life you want.

What you think, you become. What you feel, you attract. What you imagine, you create.

- Buddha

Creating A Wonderful Life

The key to creating a wonderful life is experiencing and acknowledging the longing you have to achieve your potential and live in a way that creates the true essence of who you are. Step forward into your confidence. Feel your power and your gift. Believe in your potential and worthiness.

Everyone is born with a gift. You might be a carer, a scientist, an artist, a leader, a farmer, a designer, a teacher, a protector, an architect, a builder, or a communicator. You might be good with animals, an entrepreneur, an advisor, an engineer, a musician, a philosopher, a healer, talented at technology, a writer, an organiser, a manufacturer, a mathematician, etc. The path to fulfilling your potential and experiencing the amazing gift of your life includes gaining an awareness of yourself, visualising yourself flourishing, talking about your vision, taking those necessary steps forward, and manifesting your dreams to live your best life.

1. Gaining an Awareness of You

Look at your life in the following areas:

- **Health and Well-being:** How do you want to feel in your body? What do you enjoy doing that helps you to be fit, healthy, and strong? What activities or experiences can you incorporate into your life to help you manage your thoughts and feelings, giving you good mental and emotional health? What can you do to develop a better friendship with yourself? What foods do you choose to nourish your body and mind?

- **Life Purpose and Goals:** In which area does your purpose lie? In the depths of you, what do you want to do with your life? If you don't know, think about what you loved to do when you were aged eight. Did you love to build, design, play music, perform, explore numbers, talk to people, teach others what you know, play sport, write, draw, watch and understand people's interactions, organise things, spend time with animals, do science experiments, use technology, work outside, etc.? Who did you admire growing up? What career interested you? Take back your control. You needn't blindly go into or stay in an area of work because that is what is expected of you. You can always change direction. It may take time, but it is possible to do. Take responsibility for yourself. Follow your passion. What's your identity? What are your best qualities? What are your ideas? What are you inspired to do? What are your strengths and gifts? What skills would you like to develop? What do you want to learn? What type of work or study environment would help you to achieve your potential? You have the power, strength, wisdom, and courage to bring out these gifts within yourself, fulfilling your own needs. Then, you can share these gifts with others, bringing true joy into your work, career, and family.

- **Relationship:** Would you like to welcome a new relationship into your life? Would you like to develop your relationship so that you and your partner feel more supported? What kind of relationship is in balance with your personality?

- **Family:** What would you like for your family? Would you like better relationships, deeper connections, more fun, a better understanding of personalities, fairer sharing of responsibility, favourable outcomes to difficulties, less worry?

- **Friendships:** What sort of relationships fit you well? In what kind of friendships do you thrive? Which values are important to you that you would like a friend to also value?

- **Prosperity:** What kinds of abundance would you like to receive? What material wealth do you want to welcome into your life? In what way would you like to enhance your home? Choose new experiences you would like to try; courses, travel, learning a new skill, etc.

- **Fun:** What do you like to do just for fun? What social settings do you enjoy? What activities would you like to get involved in? Where would you like to visit? What sort of people do you want to spend time with?

- **Spirituality:** Which aspects of your spiritual side would you like to develop? In what ways would you like to develop your faith? Would you like to find a new yoga, energy, tai chi, or meditation class?

2. **Visualising**

- Next, visualise yourself flourishing in all of these areas. Spend time daydreaming about each one, starting with a general feeling or concept and then slowly filling in all the details that feel good to you.

- Make a vision board as a concrete visual representation of the direction you want your life to go in. Think about your passions and imagine your future best life in all of the above areas. Write down how you would feel upon achieving that life. Then choose images and powerful words that represent your vision, making sure that each one you choose gives you a good feeling.

- Make clear intentions for a fulfilling future for yourself. Lay out your words and images in a way that pleases you, and then stick them onto a large piece of card or whiteboard.

- Frequently look at your vision board and enjoy the feeling it brings. Feel the excitement of watching your life evolve in that direction. Sometimes you will question yourself. You might question your ability or your worthiness of such a good life. Know that this is just a wobble. You need to go beyond it and get your head straight again. Steady yourself.

- Bring in positive thoughts. Trust in the power of your mind to create. Feel your best vision for yourself lining up in front of you again. Let go of the thoughts that caused you to doubt. Empower your vision. Own it.

3. Talk about your vision to people who believe in you

- Trust in yourself and your vision. Be confident in it. Talk to people you trust about your vision. Stay away from negative people. Don't let their negativity influence you or interfere with you realising your potential.

- This is about trust in yourself. Hear the declaration in your voice stating this is who you are and what you will do. This will bring you closer to manifesting your goals.

4. Take Steps

- Get the momentum going by taking steps towards your vision. Small steps are fine. Write them out. Use what you have, here and now, to start your journey. Identify your gifts, skills, ideas, and sources of support. Ask yourself, "What do I need to do this week, next week, this month, this year? What do I need to learn? Where can I learn this skill or information?"

- Keep going in your chosen direction. Take the opportunities that come your way. Make good decisions by connecting your intuition, logic, and emotions. Celebrate your success, achievements, and manifestations. Keep spending time visualising the whole picture of your vision board manifested and keep taking the next step.

5. **Manifest**

    - Enjoy experiencing your chosen life manifesting. It might not come exactly in the way you predicted it would but watch and trust. Have faith as all you want unfolds. Have confidence and follow the path you are creating. Feel the exhilaration of living in your power and the joy of the amazing gift of your life.

    Then choose again. What will you create next?

Journal Exercises

Who are you as an individual? Write about your gifts and your dreams:

My Gifts:

_____

_____

My Dreams:

_____

_____

Which of your gifts / interests drives you the most?

What is your best quality?

Use your journal to plan out your vision board.

Stepping Back - Manifesting with Vision Boards

Since my mid-teens, I have always made vision boards. My early ones were filled with drawings of how I planned my life would be. I surrounded these drawings with sketches of the Holy Spirit dove, angels, and candle flames and then I'd include a prayer. These drawings filled me with hope and gave me a feeling of protection.

In my more recent life, I make five-year vision boards with pictures and words. As I create my board and focus on my intentions, I build energy and power behind what I plan to do in the coming five years. I take time to be grateful for each step as it manifests, which puts more power behind the next piece that I am anticipating. I review my board yearly, making slight adjustments and meditating on how to help along any area that is not flowing as well as I would like. When I look back, I am amazed and filled with gratitude for the ways in which so much of the good that I have envisioned for myself on my boards has come into my life.

The Circle of Attraction Meditation

A Meditation on bringing connection, purpose, joy, and abundance into your life:

Find a comfortable and quiet place to sit. Keeping your eyes open, call your awareness back into your time and body in this space here and now. Take a piece of paper and a pen, and on it draw a circle. Divide the circle into seven parts. Write a heading on each section to represent all areas of your life, for example, health and wellbeing, life purpose and goals, primary relationship, family, friendship, prosperity and fun, and spirituality.

Close your eyes. Take a few moments to breathe deeply and allow your mind to clear and your body to relax. Allow your energy to move freely in your body and tune into positivity and having clear intentions. Open your eyes and write one thing (a word or a phrase) that you would like to be, do or have under each heading. What do you want to bring into your life? Pause and decide.

When you have chosen each area, place your piece of paper on the floor in front of you.

Feel your feet firmly on the ground. Call in the energy of beautiful scenery around you. You might call in the feeling of being in a forest, walking by the ocean, standing on a cliff, walking through a meadow, or being on an island. Picture the place clearly in your mind and feel its power travelling along the earth towards you, coming up as it reaches your feet, clearing and amplifying your energy as you ground yourself with both the energy of the earth where you are and the energy of this beautiful place. Breathe.

Visualise a column of light appearing over your head. Through this column, you are being sent loving, healing energy from above, from loved ones who have passed, from your spirit guides, from angels, from a source that highlights your presence in the universe. Honour your own faith as you visualise this limitless energy flowing into you.

As your energy gets higher, notice the sensations in and around your body. You might sense a calm stillness or a soft hum or gentle waves of vibrations rippling through your body and out your hands and feet. Feel the excitement of possibilities and your potential being realised. Imagine your energy has a brightening glow, lighting up your body and all the layers of your energy field so that you are sitting within a great big sphere of light, grounded, and connected, present and visible. Visualise a circular beam of this light shining onto the ground and onto your page. You can choose how many of your headings you'd like to work on today.

Focus on Health and Well-being:
What are you choosing to bring into your life? (As you do this visualisation, you can open your eyes and glance at your page anytime

you want.) Imagine the word or phrase that is your intention for health and well-being coming off the page and standing in mid-air in front of you. Feel the energy of your intention. What symbol or image could represent this vision for you? See the word changing into this symbol. Feel the power in it as you visualise moving the symbol, rotating it in front of you. When you are ready, draw the symbol into your body, fusing its energy with yours. Own it. Then visualise sending the symbol into the universe, simply asking it to go where it needs to so that it can come back into your life, manifesting its gift to you in the best way possible for you. Sit in gratitude.

Focus on Your Life Purpose and Goals:
Think about your life purpose and goals. What did you choose to do and achieve? What is your intention for your work? Focus on what doing this would feel like as you bring your words up off the page and change them into a symbol or picture. Feel the power and satisfaction that is there for you in this. Bring the symbol or picture into and through your energy and allow them to connect. Move your intention through your body. Own it. Send your symbol out into the universe. Trust that the path of manifestation of your life purpose and goals is now lit up for you.

Focus on Your Primary Relationship:
If you are in a relationship, what is your sincere intention for your relationship? If not, would you like to bring a new partner into your life? Imagine the word or phrase coming up from the page in your mind's eye. Choose a symbol, and as the words transform, see the symbol rotating out in front of you. Feel its essence and draw it into you, connecting it to your energy and moving it through you. Then allow it to move out from you and settle into the universe, trusting that it will soon come back to you in a way that will enhance your present relationship or bring a new one to you as you choose.

Bring Your Attention to Your Family:
What is your intention in relation to them? Bring up the words and choose your symbol. Feel the power, love, and fluidity of movement in your symbol. Allow it to move into your energy and the energy of your immediate family. See it pick up speed and move into your wider and wider family circle moving through everyone's energy. Feel its momentum grow again as it starts to move through the older and past generations of your family, moving along the branches as it touches all the ancestors with compassion and healing, slowing when it has connected to everyone it needs to. Next, see the symbol moving out in front of you, connecting with future generations with excitement and speed. Allow the symbol then to move out into the universe, ready to bring forth experiences in your life which will concretely bring into your family that which you asked. Take a moment to feel the benefit of what you have done for your family.

Focus on Friendship:
What is your intention for your friendships? Visualise bringing your word or phrase up in front of you to eye level. Choose a symbol for friendship. Look at all sides of your symbol and feel its strength and gifts for you. When you are ready, draw your symbol of friendship into your body. Feel it move through your energy and give all your attention to how this feels. Connect your energy to your symbol, and then allow it to move out into the universe and find its best place. Feel the anticipation of your intention for friendship coming into your life in ways that will surprise you.

Bring Your Attention to Your Prosperity and Fun:
What is your intention for abundance in your life in relation to both material wealth and enjoyable experiences? Bring your words of intention up off the page and out in front of you. What symbol would represent your words? See the symbol rotating in front of you. Feel the abundance and optimism in this symbol. Allow its energy to move in

and connect with yours, moving through all the layers of your energy, physical, emotional, mental, and spiritual. Next, allow the symbol to move freely out into the universe and to go to the abundance that is for you. Feel gratitude and relaxation as you sense the abundance that exists for you making its journey towards you. Trust that money and abundance is coming to you in concrete ways filling your life with joy and freedom.

Focus on Your spirituality:
What would you like to develop with regard to your spiritual side? Visualise your words rising off the page. What symbol represents this development in your spiritual potential? See this symbol in front of you and take a moment to sense its power. Draw the symbol to you to connect it with your whole energy field. Feel it as it moves through your energy. Send it out in the universe to find its place so that this new gift can find its way into your experience, and you can enjoy an expanded reality.

Visualise the energy through you and around you getting brighter with the gently swirling energy of purple, gold, and white light. See the strands of this light emanating from you connecting with all that you have asked to manifest. Enjoy this feeling.

Breathe. Feel your connection through your feet with the earth. Be grateful for all the good in your life. Trust that you are strongly attracting wonderful opportunities and experiences. Open your eyes.

Wisdom for a Good Day

- Start every day by taking a few deep breaths and checking in with your body. Feel yourself connected with the earth and imagine life-force energy coming up from the earth. Feel it in your feet and ankles coming up into your legs, stomach and organs, chest, shoulders, neck, and head, soothing you and giving you a feeling of presence, strength, courage, knowledge, and wisdom. Next, imagine a ball of white light at the base of your spine. Breathe into it, allowing it to build for 10 seconds and then allow it to travel up through your spine along each disc, feeling it pulling you together, making you strong in the present.

- Take back your control, trust, belief, and faith and live the day as it presents itself.

- Sort out your own problems as they arise and allow the people around you to sort theirs.

- Accept what you cannot change and learn to understand it.

- When you give to others, ensure it is for the right reasons and does not interfere with their learning. Give them back their control.

- Be mindful that when you overreact, you give away your control. Pause, breathe, take back your control, and feel calm.

- If you make a mistake, learn to understand it and be patient with yourself and others. Let go of guilt.

- Do not judge other people because you do not understand what their life is about and what they are dealing with in their day.

- Live in the present and be in the moment. Then you have great clarity, understanding, and compassion. Remember yesterday has gone and tomorrow is not here yet! Be present.

- Make a little time in the evening for processing your day. Sit quietly. Stop your thoughts floating by pulling yourself into your time and space in the now. Look at one thought, worry, feeling, or situation at a time. Feel the anxiety or fear or uneasy feeling. Where is it in the body? Name the feeling. Sort out which part of the feeling or situation is yours and which part belongs to another or others. Imagine handing back what doesn't belong to you. Then breathe into what is yours, fully feeling it in the here and now. Let it flow through and out of your body. Take your time with this, breathing deeply. Bring in positive words to replace the worry. Choose a colour and imagine a light of that colour flowing into your body to heal you.

Be patient with yourself as you practice bringing in this new information. You have been living a certain way for a long time, and it will take some time to change.

The Amazing Gift of Life: Key Points to Remember

- Everyone has a gift. Believe in yours and set your purpose and goals around it.

- Visualise your dreams and desires coming true and focus on the feeling of the excitement and fulfilment that everything is unfolding favourably for you.

- Vision boards are an excellent tool to help this process.

- Regularly do small things that will bring you closer to your goals.

- Send out your desires to the universe and trust and have faith that everything will work out for you.

# Part Four

Healing Practices

Practice One

Grounding

Being grounded is standing in your own power. Grounding comes from the power of your words, how you speak internally to yourself and how you speak to others. To be grounded, you need to speak true words in a tone and vibration that matches your truth. You can talk yourself into your power or out of your power. You can choose to stay in your power or give it away to others when they use their words in a way to unbalance you.

Do you speak your truth? Do you speak with integrity, staying true to your values? Are you careful with your words in how you speak to yourself and others?

Being truly grounded means being fully present. Your senses and thoughts are in the moment, here and now. You have a sense of being connected to the ground beneath your feet, a sense of space, 360 degrees around your body. You know who you are, your strengths and weaknesses, and you feel centred in that knowing. You own your life experiences and practice taking the positive learning from the more difficult ones. You have built or refined a structure for yourself of your beliefs, values, and purpose. You can stay in your own power in your family setting, at school, at work, and with friends.

We don't tend to stay fully grounded in our day-to-day life. Our own thoughts and words, other people, busy environments, stressful or sad times pull us out of our connection to our true selves. And that's okay. The key is to recognise when you are grounded, and then you can notice when you are not and work on re-grounding yourself.

But what works for you to help you ground yourself? Is it meditation, breathing deeply, listening to music, playing music, visualisation such as imagining roots connecting you to the earth, walking on the beach, spending time in a forest, gardening, walking barefoot, going outside in the rain, taking time for yourself to draw or watch a good movie, eating a good dinner, having a cup of tea, reading, lying on your bed, chatting to a grandparent, building something, playing, or doing some physical exercise? Do you feel more grounded during days that have a very structured routine or a less structured one? Once you know what works for you, you'll find it easier to re-enter a grounded state.

Be love, be one, be joy, be hope, be true, and honest. I am who I am.

I am taking back my control, trust, belief, and faith in myself.

Grounding Exercise

For this exercise, sit, lie, or stand comfortably. Breathe in and out. Take back your control. Focus on your trust, belief, and faith in yourself. Become aware of the physical structure of your body and your current emotions. Gently clear your mind allowing thoughts to flow in and out with as little attachment to them as you can.

- Visualise vibrant life-force energy in the ground beneath you. Imagine it moving in through your feet, ankles, knees, and up your legs. Allow it to move into your pelvis, tailbone, and sacrum. Hold the energy that is flowing up your legs in your sacrum. Let the energy build here for a count of five. Then release it and allow it to move up along your back from disc to disc, pulling you together into the present time. Feel solid within yourself. Breathe. Continue the flow of energy out the top of your head.

Divine Energy Insight, Healing and Potential

- Now focus again more deeply on the feet and feel or imagine energy flowing into your feet, your ankles, lower legs, knees, your thighs, pelvis, hips, all of the organs in the lower and upper abdomen, your heart, the back of your heart, your lungs, ribs, breastbone, shoulders, arms, your elbows and hands, your throat, face, all of the sensory organs, your nose, ears, eyes, brain and out the top of the head, allowing the energy to relax your muscles and to correct your circulation.

- Visualise your spiritual connection above your head. Imagine beautiful white energy coming down into the top of your head, flowing down into your brain and face, down through your throat, heart, collar bone, chest, breastbone, into your shoulders, arms, and hands, into your solar plexus, lower abdomen, base, legs, and out your feet.

- Continue this energy flow. Breathe in, connecting with earth-energy in through your feet, upwards into the legs, tailbone, pelvis, abdomen, chest, shoulders, through your hands and arms, throat, and out your head. Connect with spiritual energy, then breathe out, bringing it down through your head, throat, heart, chest, stomach, base, legs, out your feet, and connecting with the earth. Keep the flow going. As you breathe in, connect your feet with the earth, allow energy to go up through the whole body, breathing out connecting to the energy above. Energy flows in through the top of your head and down through the whole body. Keep breathing deeply and slowly and allow the flow to continue.

- Create a bubble of space 360 degrees around you. Expand the flow of energy to fill your space. Visualise protective pillars of light surrounding your space. Choose a protective colour for its outer layer, maybe green, pink, or purple. Fill yourself and your space with positive words. "I accept myself. I am courageous. I am kind. I am strong. Everything is okay. I can take the learning from situations and let go of what is not good for my well-being. I own my own identity and power. I am who I am. I am true to myself."

- Fill yourself with gratitude for all the achievements of your life.
- Own your place in life.
- Own your space around you and allow everyone else to own theirs.
- Feel your connection and power.
- Feel your presence in the moment.

Practice Two

Five Finger Breathing

The *Five Finger Breathing Exercise* is a simple mindfulness technique and guided practice used for focus, strengthening our ability to calm our body and mind. This breath work helps to anchor our concentration and connect us with the present moment.

- Hold out your left hand. Brush the side of the left wrist and hand with the fingers of your right hand.

- Breathe in deeply, tracing the side of the little finger of the left hand with the pointer finger of your right hand. Touch the top of the little finger and hold your breath. Breathe out slowly, tracing down the inside of your little finger.

- Breathe in deeply, tracing the side of the ring finger of the left hand with the pointer finger of the right hand. Hold the breath while touching the top of the ring finger, and then release the breath slowly as you trace the inside of the ring finger.

- Continue breathing and tracing along the side of the middle finger, index finger, and thumb of the left hand and then brush down along the other side of your left hand and wrist. Place your right hand over your left wrist and grip it firmly, feeling your connection to the present.

- Repeat on the same hand or swap hands.

Practice Three

The Calm Breath

You will have come across *The Calm Breath* earlier in the book. I have included it here also to encourage its daily use. It's a cornerstone practice. As a reminder, the calm breath work helps you create your own definite space around you so that you can be yourself, feel your own power, and feel protected from being overwhelmed by the thoughts and emotions of others around you. It is done at a moderate pace using some force with the out-breath, resulting in internal calm.

- Imagine there is a membrane surrounding your body that contains your life-force energy. It is quite close to your body.

- Breathe in a deep breath through your nose for a count of three and breathe out through the mouth for a count of five, pushing the membrane a little bit away from your body, 360 degrees around you.

- Feel a sense of space and stillness around you for a moment.

- Breathe in again for a count of three. Breathe out for the count of five, expanding the space all around you. Pause to feel the space and stillness for a moment.

- Do this a number of times until you feel your body relaxing, making sure after the out-breaths to sweep the calm feeling all around your body.

- Feel how you have changed the energy and atmosphere around you.

- Feel inside your feet and your connection with the earth to ground yourself.

- Feel your own power and how clearly you can see what is going on in the present moment. Notice how much quieter your mind has become.

- Feel your access to your logic and reasoning as you sit or stand calmly in your space.

Practice Four

The Rope of Life

The *Rope of Life Meditation* is a great process for healing your past and freeing you to let go of the emotional, mental, and physical weight of past experiences. Doing this meditation frequently, sorting out one or two memories each time, will bring about great healing for you. It also provides a focus for being mindful in the present and allows you to set intentions in place for your future.

To begin, close your eyes, sit comfortably, and take a few slow, deep breaths. Visualise a rope going through the centre of your body. See the rope coming out of your body at the front and then going out behind you. The purpose of this rope is to act as a visual structure for your life. Visualise how the rope in front of you holds your future, the rope behind you holds your past, and the rope going through your centre holds your present.

Feel the sensations of this in your body. Do you feel pulled to the left or the right? Do you have a sense of falling backwards or forwards? Do you feel a little dizzy? Concentrate and listen to your body. What sensations do you feel? Where in your body do you feel it?

Breathe and trust that whatever comes up does so in order to be resolved.

The Rope of Life Part One - Your Past

Focus on the rope behind you. Visualise your past as being stored chronologically along this rope. Your most recent experiences are stored closest to you, and your earliest experiences are stored furthest away. You can imagine each age of your life has a section for storing all experiences that happened at that age. It is easy to carry your past when it is stored in such a way.

Some of your memories have not yet been stored in their place. Some are stored too close to you. These are the ones that frequently intrude on your thoughts and may come with strong feelings that you struggle with. What memory comes up for you now? What comes up through your thoughts? What emotions are entwined in this memory? You are carrying the impact of this memory in your body. Where do you feel it? What conclusion or decision had you come to about this experience that keeps you stuck?

Instead of judging yourself or others very harshly, stand back a little and look at what you learned from this experience? What wisdom did you gain? What strength did it develop in you? What lesson did you learn from it? Decide to take the good from this experience. Take ownership of the positives. Breathe into the rest of it and let it go, releasing the strong emotion, releasing the opinions. Breathe and feel the difference in your body. Ask the memory to go and take its proper position on the rope and visualise it settling in its correct place.

Other memories have been pushed too far back on the rope. When this happens, we are trying to hide memories so we can protect ourselves from them. While we do not think about them very often, they give us a general feeling of unease and anxiety. We can sometimes have a prickly nature as we defend ourselves against interactions with others that may trigger them.

Allow one of these memories to surface. There is no need to pressurise yourself into bringing it up too clearly. No analysis is needed.

Gently ask yourself to allow all the information of this memory to come together, thoughts, emotions, and physical sensations. Breathe into it for three breaths. Visualise sending the emotions and thoughts of others you entwined with this memory back to them. Visualise a white healing light going in through your heart and flowing to the part of your body that needs healing from this memory. Feel the strength this light gives you. Imagine writing a positive message for yourself and putting it into the part of your body that needs it. Flow more healing light into the memory and send it to settle into its correct place on your rope.

Come back to your centre and core, into the here and now, and centre yourself back to the present. Breathe in and out gently, acknowledging what you have healed. Stand up and feel rooted and grounded. Breathe deeply, allowing your head to clear, your emotions to settle and ease to flow through your entire physical body.

The Rope of Life Part Two - Your Present

Focus on the section of the rope going through the centre of your body. Become aware of how this section of the rope feels. Allow the rope to anchor you into the present. Feel your power in this piece of the rope. Feel your presence. Here, you are connected to your intuition, values, and complete control, trust, belief, and faith. In this space, honour your true personality, your goodness, and your creativity. Acknowledge the power of your gifts and strengths. Breathe gently and be one with yourself.

The Rope of Life Part Three - Your Future

Look at your rope of life in front of you. What does it look like? Is it strong or weak? Are you comfortable with your future? Are you afraid of it? Does it fill you with panic and anxiety? Are you excited about your future? What life purpose, plans, and goals have you set out on the rope for your future? Is your rope heading directly straight out in front of you, or is it pulled to one side?

Breathe and take back your control from your parents, siblings, friends, teachers, and extended family. Feel what changes in your rope and acknowledge it.

Visualise a golden healing light coming down, in through the top of your head, flowing down through your forehead, throat, heart and chest, upper abdomen, lower abdomen and pelvis, and into your arms and legs. Enjoy the sensation of this healing light flowing through and around your body. As this golden light continues to flow, direct it out of your centre along the rope in front of you. Visualise holding the rope. Allow healing, self-acceptance, courage, and strength to flow along the rope. See it thickening and strengthening, keeping a little flexibility in it. Let go of others' opinions. Let go of critical thoughts and let go of basing your future on your past. Your future is a new creation. Place a sense of your power and identity into the rope. Take responsibility for your life. Own your own rope. Look at the goals and plans you have on your rope and trust your gut by letting go of any which are not true to who you are. Organise everything else by placing them in sequential order along the rope. Spend some time setting out more goals and plans for your next six months, your next year. Send strength and self-belief into the rope as you place each one. Infuse your values and your sense of your life purpose into the rope to assist you as you move forward.

Remember to acknowledge that there will be some dips and bends in the rope as you experience life lessons along the way. After each dip, decide to gather up the learning, let go of what you need to and raise the level of the rope again. Set an intention to regularly flow healing light along your rope to keep your desired future vibrant and strong. Spend a few moments feeling the excitement of the adventure of your life goals and purpose manifesting. Bring in a feeling of gratitude.

Centre yourself back into the here and now, acknowledging your vision for your future. Trust what you have done. Be grounded. Visualise a ball of light in the bottom of your back. Allow it to move up along your backbone, pulling you together in the here and now. Then, when you are ready, slowly open your eyes and feel grounded.

Practice Five

The Bubble Meditation

The *Bubble Meditation* will guide you to a sense of connection with yourself and create a spherical layer of protection around your energy. This practice can also help us become aware of our energy's frequency as it flows through us.

Visualise a bubble all around you. You are inside the bubble, and you are safe and well protected. Now fill your bubble with a colour. Choose a colour to help you feel relaxed and calm. Breathe in and out, in and out, in and out, quick breaths. Take in a deep breath, hold for a count of two to three, and release totally. Repeat for four more breaths. Using one hand, pat each of the following parts of your body eight times at a slow, gentle rhythm:

- Start by patting your forehead.
- Next, gently pat your throat.
- Now pat your heart.
- Pat your upper abdomen.
- Pat your lower abdomen.
- Next, pat your hips.

Divine Energy Insight, Healing and Potential

- Pat your knees.
- Lastly, gently stamp your feet eight times, being aware of how your feet touch the ground.

You may start feeling a vibration moving up your body through your feet and legs into your pelvis, stomach, chest, heart, throat, and out through the top of your head. Along with this sensation, visualise your life-force energy moving into your hands, up your arms, into your shoulders, into your neck, and out through your head. Visualise a ball of light moving into your tailbone and up to the top of your spine, pulling you into your present time here and now, protecting you and healing you.

Breathe nice and gentle to relax the body. Tune in to your body and acknowledge how you are feeling now within this bubble of protection.

Practice Six

Healing Meditation for our Bones

When we want or need to soothe and relax our bodies, we generally focus on our muscles and organs. This meditation will focus on our often neglected bones, in which we also store our pain. Our bones do amazing work for us. Our skeleton is a supportive frame that gives our body shape, allows us to stand upright and gives us our physical structure. It protects our organs from impact, and together with our muscles, our bones allow our body to move in extraordinarily complex ways.

There is much life-force and activity going on inside our bones as most red and white blood cells are made in our bone marrow. Our bones also act as storage areas for important minerals, releasing them as our body requires. The suppressed thoughts, feelings, and pain we store in our bones are often very deep-rooted ones, such as trauma. Pain, suffering, rigidness, and negative beliefs carried down through the generations in our families can be stored in our bones. We also carry day to day pressures, burdens, hardship, and tiredness in our bones.

For this meditation, sit or lie comfortably. Close your eyes and allow your breathing to settle into a slow, even rhythm with your heart and body.

Divine Energy Insight, Healing and Potential

- Ground yourself by focusing inside your feet and feeling your connection to the earth.

- Become aware of your bones. How do your bones feel? Do they feel heavy or light? Strong or fragile? Do they feel as if they fit well together or not? Do the bones on each side of your body feel equal in size? Do you feel soreness, tiredness, pain, or aches in any of your bones? Do you feel balanced? Does your skeleton have a weak spot that gets achy when you have a tough day?

- Visualise your skeleton in your mind's eye, becoming aware of your backbone from the top of your spine down to your sacrum. Does it feel strong or weak? Visualise giving your spine some power.

- How does your skull feel? Where do you feel pressure or pain? Breathe in and on the out-breath, imagine more space around your brain and the plates of your skull releasing the discomfort. Breathe in ease and space. Become aware of the frontal bone of your skull. Other people's negativity and drama can bring an agitated feeling to your forehead. Breathe in and on the out-breath, let go of any agitation. Breathe in peace and clarity.

- Become aware of the bones in your face. What are you holding in your jawbones? Do you often clench your jaws with anger or resentment or when you are internalising information? Breathe in and on the out-breath, release all tension from your jaws. Feel new ease and comfort in your jaws.

- Focus on your cheekbones. Do they feel tender? We often store the hurtful comments thrown at us in our cheekbones. Breathe in and out, releasing tenderness from your cheekbones. Breathe in a feeling of safety into this area.

- Bring your attention to your ears. How does the soft cartilage of your ears feel? Become aware of your inner ear bones? What have you not wanted to hear that is still stored in your ear cartilage and bones? Breathe in and on the out-breath, let go of these upsets from your ears. Imagine listening to a sound that soothes your ears, such as relaxing music or ocean waves. Feel the waves of vibration moving through your ears.

- Become aware of the bones in your neck. How do you hold your neck? What incidents have hit you in the neck? What shocks have jolted your neck? What threats have you stored in the back of your neck? Whatever comes up for you, breathe into it and release it. Repeat for two more breaths. Breathe in a feeling of comfort.

- Focus on your shoulder bones. What burdens have you taken onto your shoulders? Breathe in and on the out-breath, release the weight of burdens off your shoulders. Breathe in a feeling of lightness and freedom. Become aware of your shoulder blades and the hollow between your shoulder blades. We often store emotions here. Breathe in and on the out-breath, release any suppressed emotions, feeling your shoulders relax.

- Bring your attention to your collarbone. We store tension and pressure on this long horizontal bone. Breathe and release any pressure you feel in this bone. Breathe in ease and relax your collarbone.

- Become aware of the long bones in your right arm, of your elbow, your wrist, your hand, and your fingers. Your arms allow you to express yourself in a negative or positive way via your body language and actions. What have you held in your arm bones and not expressed? Notice any pain, pressure, or discomfort. Breathe in and then release what you want to let go of on the out-breath.

- Become aware of the long bones in your left arm, your left elbow, your wrist, your hand, and your fingers. Notice any pain, pressure, or discomfort. What have you stored in the bones of your left arm? Breathe in and release what you want to let go of with the out-breath.

- Focus on your ribs. Our ribs are where we tend to store anger, resentment, hurt, or betrayal. What do you feel in your ribs? Breathe in and breathe out old, suppressed emotions from your ribs. Breathe in forgiveness and peace of mind.

- Become aware of your spine and all of its discs. Your backbone holds you together. How does your spine feel? Our spines become weakened when we don't believe in ourselves and when we feel depressed. Breathe in and on the out-breath release self-doubt, sadness, and negative thoughts from your spine. Breathe in self-belief and enthusiasm about your life and your potential.

- Bring your attention to your pelvis, your left and right hip, and hip joints. Become aware of what is holding you back in your life and of your life's hardships that have impacted your hips and pelvis? How do these bones feel? Do you feel any soreness, stiffness, or pain? Breathe in and on the out-breath, release restriction, despair, and resentment from these bones.

- Become aware of the long bones in your left leg, your left knee and kneecap, your ankle, your foot bones, and your toes. Notice any pain, pressure, or discomfort. Do your legs feel tired, have low energy, feel achy or cramp frequently? Do you have problems with your left foot? Your feet store all the information about your life experiences. You may have stored what you don't want to feel in your legs and feet. Breathe in and then release what you want to let go of with the out-breath.

- Become aware of the long bones in your right leg, your right knee and kneecap, your ankle, your foot bones and your toes. Notice any pain, pressure, or discomfort. Do you have problems with your right foot? Breathe in and then release what you want to let go of, achiness, tiredness, suppressed emotion, and anything that makes you feel stuck with the out-breath.

- Imagine beautiful light over your head. Bring the light down into your body to heal and balance your skeleton. Imagine the healing light moving into the soft bone marrow of all your bones, all the way through to the tougher outer layers of the bones. If you have had a hip or knee replacement, run the energy through the artificial joint also. If you have had an amputation, still visualise the energy running through both limbs so that you can feel the full symmetry of your skeletal system energetically.

- Visualise healing energy lighting up your skull and forehead, your cheekbones and jaws, your ears, your neck, shoulders and shoulder blades, your collar bone, arms and hands, your breastbone, ribs, spine, pelvis and hips, your legs, knees, ankles, and feet. Allow the light to flow out of the bottom of your feet, anchoring you to the ground and allow it to flow around your body.

- Feel your feet grounded and rooted. Be present. Be here. Be now.

- Acknowledge what is released from your skeleton, allowing your muscle to relax in a new way and your circulation to flow with ease.

Practice Seven

Loving Heart Meditation

Healing our heart from the life experiences which have left a hurtful echo allows us to bring compassion, balance, and harmony into our lives. *The Loving Heart Meditation* guides us to listen to and honour the memories of our heart, encouraging us to practice self-compassion and to bring loving energy to soothe and heal our heart.

To begin this meditation, become aware of your body as you sit in a chair or lie down. Come into your full presence, here and now, in this moment of time, your time.

- Bring your attention to your heart. How do you feel inside your heart? Your heart has a powerful and constant rhythm. Place your hand over your heart and feel its beat. The rhythm of your heart can pull all of the body's systems into harmony. A calm, steady heartbeat makes a calm, balanced body.

- Allow your heart to open. Feel your love connection to yourself. With your inner voice, say caring things to yourself.

- Feel your love connection to other people. Imagine love from your heart travelling along invisible, individual strings to the hearts of people that you love. Allow love to travel from their heart back to yours.

- Acknowledge the emotions of your heart, your current emotions and those you have stored in your heart throughout your life. Acknowledge the emotions that come up for you to be healed and released now. Is it hurt, grief, disconnection, regret, sadness, fright, worry about loved ones, rejection, or betrayal?

- Take a few deep breaths and create some space for yourself, in front of you, behind you, either side of you, above, and below you. Look at the sensitivity of your own heart from the time of its first beat in the womb, right up to the present time, here and now. Ask yourself to sit with care, love, courage, wisdom, and knowledge as you think about all your life experiences from your heart's point of view. From within the womb, as a baby, as a young child, an older child, as a teenager, all the way up to your present age.

- What emotions have you stored in your heart that you would like to clear now? Begin to flow your attention through your ages, feeling your heart at each stage of your life. Pause at each age, breathe, and feel the most prevalent emotion that is felt by your heart, breathe into stored emotion, and acknowledge it. Give your heart love, compassion, and care as you move through every age.

- You may remember people, situations, and old feelings from your life at each stage. Hold onto the love you felt and decide to let go of anything that doesn't serve you well in your life today. You may feel some sensations throughout your body and not just in your heart. Breathe into these feelings and release them.

- Continue to flow your attention into your heart, keep counting through all the ages, right up to the present time. Take your time, going through each age, not spending too long at any particular one.

- Place your hand on your heart and give it love and care. Decide to declutter the heart of all the experiences that have upset you.

- Acknowledge any hurt you have stored in your heart. If an incident where you felt hurt by someone comes to mind, ask yourself to take a step back and see what was happening for the other person and notice how they may not have been coping well at the time with their own emotions and you were hurt as a result. In your mind's eye, visualise yourself handing back the emotion they off-loaded onto you. Imagine a green healing light soothing away the hurt you felt.

- Acknowledge any grief that is stored in your heart. For a moment, just allow love to flow between you and who you grieve for. Ask yourself what support you need to handle your grief, and promise yourself you will seek this support. Imagine a healing green light flowing through your heart and in and out through the back of your heart, comforting you.

- Acknowledge times in your life when you have felt disconnected. Strengthen your connection with yourself by affirming your abilities, values, and goals. Imagine a pink healing light warming your heart filling it with a feeling of self-acceptance.

- Acknowledge any regrets you have stored in your heart. Connect the emotions of your heart with kind, logical thoughts. Accept your regret as something that happened because of where you were at that time. Take the learning from the situation with you and release the guilt. Nurture your heart with green healing light.

- Acknowledge any sadness or disappointment you have held onto. Choose an event in your life that caused you to feel sadness or disappointment. Accept the feeling. Don't push it away. This may not be a feeling you would choose, but when you sit with it and breathe into it, it has a jewel for you, a knowing, a new direction, a discovery about yourself, a learning. Take in this positive with gratitude and let go of the sadness.

- Acknowledge any fright that is still stored in your heart. Sometimes when a sudden trauma occurs, we can feel a sudden impact on the heart. Place your hand on your heart and imagine pink and green energy clearing this shock from your heart. Reassure yourself that this fright is in the past, and it's ok to stop replaying this event in your mind and to let go of the imprint this shock has made on you.

- Acknowledge the worry in your heart about loved ones. If it relates to the past, release it. If it is an ongoing situation, commit to regularly grounding yourself, taking back your control, trust, faith, and belief. Practise *The Calm Breath* to give you a feeling of space, separating your emotions from theirs and giving back what does not belong to you. Decide on the support you can give to this person while lightly holding the responsibility you feel towards them. Love them, hold a vision of the best possible future for them and daydream in this vision instead of thinking fearfully and negatively.

- Acknowledge any stored feelings of rejection or betrayal. When you hold onto the pain of rejection or betrayal in your heart, it is only because when someone rejected or betrayed you, you also rejected or betrayed yourself by agreeing with them on some level. Place your hand on your heart and give it love, care, and compassion. Say kind things to yourself, affirming your goodness, value, and worth. Imagine pink healing light mending your heart from all rejection and betrayal. Imagine this healing light filling your heart with acceptance, tolerance, and peace.

- Acknowledge how lighter your heart feels as you let go of all that accumulated emotion.

- Honour the sensitivity of your heart. If there was a window to the emotions of your heart, what would you see if you looked in now? Visualise sending healing to the parts of your heart that have been broken. Visualise filling in any cracks with beautiful healing light.

- Imagine a back door in your heart. Open it for a moment and sweep out any remaining heaviness or emptiness. Then imagine flooding your heart with compassion, contentment, affection, joy, peace, courage, healing, and love.

- Acknowledge your gifts, abilities, goals, and qualities. Bring in self-acceptance, trust, faith, and belief in yourself. Feel it in your heart. Take back your control from others. Think, "I am who I am, I am."

- Feel your connection with your own heart and your loved ones' hearts, the unconditional, simple, powerful love flowing from you and to you.

- Bring your attention to your feet and feel your connection with the earth.

- Visualise a strong connection between your heart and your gut, allowing your heart's emotions to have immediate access to the wisdom and protection of your intuition. Simultaneously visualise a strong connection between your heart and your brain, allowing your heart's emotions to have access to the logic and reasoning of your mind. Your feelings, logic, and knowing are properly aligned, informing each other as needed.

- Observe your heart beating with a slow, constant, steady rhythm, and as it does so, observe how all your bodily systems harmonise and come into balance.

Practice Eight
Healing Lungs Meditation

Breathing connects us to our life-force energy. Tuning into our breath brings us awareness and presence. Breathing deeply into our lungs allows us to increase the life-force that we take in. It calms us, strengthens our immune system, improves our ability to concentrate and encourages us to think more positively. Breathing out with presence and focus allows us to let go of emotions and thoughts that we have stored, which would be best released. We tend to hold onto sadness, suffocation, hurt, resentment, and grief in our lungs. This meditation brings a powerful healing to your chest and encourages the exchange that occurs in the lungs back into balance.

To begin, find a quiet space to sit comfortably. Relax in your body. Feel your feet touching the ground and your connection with the earth.

- Gently close your eyes and focus on your breathing for a few moments, becoming aware of the movement of your breath. How does it feel? Does it feel deep or shallow, free, or tight, clear, or restricted?

- Breathe in for a count of four, hold for a few seconds and breathe out for a count of four. Repeat for five more breaths.

- Keep your attention on your lungs. Deep breathing involves filling all of both lungs by allowing the diaphragm to drop downwards and the ribcage to expand outwards, creating lots of space for the lungs to inflate. Feel your lungs expanding and contracting as you continue to breathe in and out slowly. Stay with this for a few moments.

- Visualise your lungs as you inhale, bringing oxygen into your body and as you exhale, releasing carbon dioxide. Focus on breathing in oxygen and out carbon dioxide. Acknowledge the vital role your lungs play, bringing into your body what you need and letting go of what is no longer needed.

- Your lungs work in this way day and night, exchanging air, in and out, in and out, bringing in and letting go.

- Become aware that your lungs work in a similar way, taking in emotions and letting them go.

- The ebb and flow of our emotions are connected with the ebb and flow of our breath. Sometimes we flow with the dance of our emotions, breathing in and feeling our emotions and on the out-breath, letting them move through us and out. Other times we resist the flow and let the troublesome feelings we don't want to feel remain stuck in our body.

- Become aware of your lungs, left and right. Breathe gently for a few moments. What have you stored in your lungs that you could now release? Do you feel any uncomfortable physical sensations in your lungs, tightness, pressure, restriction, or pain? What old emotions have you stored in your lungs? What have you tried to avoid feeling? What have you not fully processed, sadness, suffocation, hurt, resentment, or grief? What old beliefs have you stored in your lungs, hardened attitudes and opinions, old ways of living that no longer serve you?

- Be aware of what's changing in your lungs.

- Ask your thoughts not to focus on any particular emotion or belief that comes up for you.

- Sit and be present for a few moments with all of the feelings coming up within you for healing. Trust in the capability of your lungs to clear, filter, and heal all that you have stored.

- Become aware of the power of your connection to the earth.

- Bring up life-force energy through your feet, up your legs into your pelvis, feeling a surge of energy in this area.

- Allow it to build for a few moments as it moves slowly but gently through the body filling the lungs with this beautiful green healing energy. Stay with this for a few moments feeling its power and strength.

- Visualise a beautiful green energy filling your whole body. Allow the energy to continue to flow up and out through the top of the head, connecting you in a much stronger way with source energy.

- Way above your head, visualise a flame coming to you from source energy. It flickers with white, gold, blue, and green. Visualise it coming down through the top of your head, slowly moving down through the body into the lungs. See it illuminating the trachea, the bronchi, the alveoli, and the diaphragm.

- Feel the heat of this flame of transformation blazing in your lungs. Feel it in your left lung, right down in the bottom of your lung and filling your whole left lung. Feel the flame in your right lung, right down in the bottom of your lung and filling your whole right lung. Feel the power of this flame burning blue as it transforms the old stale emotions and beliefs.

- Acknowledge the power of this healing for a few moments. Breathe deeply in and out, emptying the lungs of all that is being cleared on the out-breaths. Relax in your breathing for a couple of minutes and give yourself time to feel gratitude for the healing that has taken place in your lungs.

- Become aware of your heart, asking the energy from the healing flame to radiate in and around your heart. Visualise the flow of energy connecting from the lungs to the heart and the heart to the lungs working together in harmony.

- Allow the energy to flow into your shoulders, down the arms and out through your fingertips.

- Focus back into your chest. Send the energy down into your stomach around the abdominal organs, into your pelvis and hips and down your legs out through your feet.

- Visualise the energy in your chest and see it moving into the breastbone and collarbone, up into the throat and neck, into your face and head and out through the top of your head.

- Move the energy all around your energy field.

- Feel safe, protected, calm, grounded, and connected with self. Feel the power of your presence in this moment.

Practice Nine

Deep Meditation

With your eyes gently closed, take a deep breath. Slowly let it out, relaxing your lungs and chest. Breathe deeply into your stomach. Let each breath take you into a beautiful state of relaxation. As you breathe, feel lighter and lighter and go deeper and deeper into relaxation.

Your body feels lighter and lighter as you go deeper and deeper again into a beautiful state of relaxation. Your body is relaxing. Imagine you are breathing beautiful energy within you and around you. Relax your breathing to the rhythm of your heart, allow each breath to relax you and breathe out any tension or stress in the body for fifteen seconds.

- Now bring up your energy. Feel the energy flow into the bottom of your feet and into your ankles, calves, knees, thighs, and pelvis moving from your left hip to your right hip, relaxing all the muscles and the circulation in the body.

- Become aware of your hands. Feel the energy move into the left hand, elbow, and shoulder. Repeat the same into your right hand, elbow, and shoulder, relaxing all the muscles and circulation in the body.

- Focus back on your pelvis and allow the energy to flow into the centre of your lower abdomen. This area holds your gut feelings. Allow the energy to build up, opening up your intuition for ten seconds.

- Feel the energy move into your stomach, filling it with peace, love, light, and healing. Allow the energy to continue to flow from the stomach into your chest, into your heart, the back of your heart, into your throat, the back of the throat, your face, and head, and allowing it to move out through the top of your head, raising your energy and vibrations.

- Now focus back on your tailbone and lower back. Hold the energy here, allowing it to build up tenfold, twenty-fold, thirty-fold, forty-fold and then release it, letting it move along each disc up the back, to the top of the spine, into your shoulders and neck, the back of the head and out through the top of your head raising your energy and vibrations and relaxing all the muscles in the body, correcting circulation, and muscle, touching every fibre, cell, and organ in your body with peace, love, light, and healing.

- Let go of focusing on any outside noises. Let them just take you deeper into a beautiful state of relaxation.

- Visualise or feel a beautiful light above your head. This healing light of energy will deepen your relaxation and heal your body. Let the light flow into your body down through the top of your head. It illuminates the brain and spinal cord, healing these tissues and deepening your level of relaxation even more. Let the healing light flow down from above through your body like a beautiful wave of light touching every cell, fibre, and organ in your body with peace, love, light, and healing. Allow the energy to be stronger in your lower abdomen.

Divine Energy Insight, Healing and Potential

- Wherever your body needs energy, let the light be stronger and more powerful in this area and let the light flow to your feet so that your body is filled with this beautiful healing light and energy.

- Now imagine or feel the light completely surrounding the body as if wrapped in a beautiful bubble. This protects you and deepens your level even more.

- In this wonderful state of peace and tranquillity, imagine yourself walking down beautiful steps. Counting backwards from ten to one, let each number take you deeper and deeper into a more relaxed state.

Ten	-	Lighter, lighter, deeper, and deeper
Nine	-	Down deeper and deeper
Eight	-	Down with each step, lighter and deeper with each number
Seven	-	More peaceful and relaxed
Six	-	More and more at peace and relaxed
Five	-	More and more relaxed
Four	-	More relaxed and calmer, calmer, and calmer
Three	-	Calm, lighter and lighter, and lighter
Two	-	Peace in your mind, love in your heart, and healing in your body
One	-	Relax

- As you reach the bottom of the steps, imagine a beautiful place of sanctuary, a garden, a beach, a forest, wherever you feel most comfortable. Walk into your place of sanctuary and find a place to rest.

- Your body is still filled by light and surrounded by the light. This continues to heal you.

- Open up your intuition which is found in your lower abdomen. Remember, you are always in control and have your trust, belief, and faith within yourself.

- Your body in this space is now filled with beautiful light. It is healing and refreshing you. Allow your presence to fill this place. Take some time here to reflect. Be still and quiet and take in what's around you. This is your sanctuary, a place to relax and reflect for a few minutes on what is going on within you and around you, a space where you can be fully present within you. What loving message do you have for yourself here? Give yourself a couple of moments to take in this information.

- When you are ready, visualise yourself standing up and walking out of the space you have created. See the steps in front of you, counting from one to ten. With each number, bring yourself back to the here and now.

- Going up each step, 1, 2, 3 feeling relaxed, refreshed, lighter, and lighter.

- 4, 5, 6, more aware and alert. Feeling great.

- 7, 8, more at peace and calm. Nearly awake now.

- 9, 10, open your eyes slowly. You will experience more clarity, and your eyes will feel lighter and brighter, awake and alert.

- Take your time, stretch, and relax.

- Feel your body. Relax and be aware of your surroundings and feel grounded in the present.

A Final Note

Engaging with the ideas in this book will guide you to a place where life begins to flow more easily for you. In this place, you will find managing your thoughts, releasing stored emotions, and easing pain in your body, is a much easier process than it once was. Using the practices we've discussed, following the meditations, and finding the power of your breath, will give you the strength and belief in yourself to manage your day. You will uncover many truths, ease blockages, and confront thoughts in a way that will bring you to know who you are, releasing the power you have had all along to create your future.

Of course, every so often, something comes up in life, a change or a challenge which can unsettle even the most at ease individual. Upsets can leave you feeling overwhelmed and powerless. You may even think all the work you've done has slipped through your fingers, and you are back to square one. You're not, and thinking in this way is normal. Remember, it's okay. With understanding and care, you will get yourself through any difficult period of life because you have the tools to do so. Pause so you can take the time to look at the situation objectively. Talk kindly and compassionately to yourself, and you will come out of the turbulence of negative thinking. Detach from the drama and take back your power by giving back to others what isn't yours to be taking on. Flow healing energy through your body, releasing what needs to go and breathing in strength, love, and light.

Let's remember to consolidate the love that is out there for us and our beliefs which keep us strong, keep us going through every tricky and demanding time in our life and all the way out to the other side. When we prioritise what needs to be done as we go through tough days, we can let go of what is unnecessary to give ourselves some space and time to care for what is important within us. And never overlook the value of a keen sense of humour. Every drama has its funny side. A sense of humour is a great comfort.

I understand life can throw us challenges that can leave us questioning, fearful, and hurt. But I also understand that we are strong and resilient despite our vulnerabilities. So be brave, as I know you can be when making decisions for yourself. We have the choice and free will to make incredibly positive changes for our future. Make goals for yourself based on what you would love to do, be or have in your life and then own your road to them. Make it yours. Let go of doubt. Bring in faith and knowing. Be focused on your thoughts about achieving what you set out to do and spend time feeling the excitement of manifestation before your goals are fulfilled. This mindset will encourage you to take the opportunities that come your way, and if something doesn't flow well, don't panic. Tweak things a bit, find ways around the obstacle's life puts before you, and find new routes that flow more easily to your desired outcome. Keep your intentions and information clear by not allowing others to interfere and truly allow your potential to be realised.

This is your journey, your life. Every day take ownership of yourself. Own your inner strengths, qualities, values, optimism, power, wisdom, knowledge, and wit. Believe in what you have to offer yourself and others. Honour your self-worth and see the value of your full presence in the world and the difference your kindness can make to other people. Step out and bring your gifts into the world because you have an essential role, a big part to play in life. Stand in your grounded connection to life and fully live the adventure. Everything is okay.

By knowing yourself, living as yourself, being at home in yourself, and sharing your gifts, you will find contentment, peace, love, joy, and fulfilment beyond your imaginings.

Divine Energy: Key Points to Remember

- Do not fear looking at your life and expressing what you really feel. When you let go of this fear you begin to truly live.

- You have free will and you can change your future based on the choices that you make in your present.

- Your thoughts affect your health. Take back your control, trust, belief, and faith in yourself and choose to think in a positive way.

- Trust your intuition. Check in with your gut feeling. Your first thought that comes to you is the correct answer. Trust yourself.

- Don't be afraid of life but instead believe that it is worth living. This belief will help you create your future.

- When you achieve an understanding and acceptance of your true self, you will gain the strength, courage, and confidence to live life in the present.

- There is no greater joy than knowing you are a real and unique person. Find yourself, be yourself, and as you get a greater understanding of yourself, you will find peace and balance. Happiness comes from being connected with your true self.

Resources

If you are in need of support, reach out and ask for help. This list is a sample of the many organisations in Ireland working to give emotional support and practical help to us during difficult times:

	Organisation:	Website:	Phone:	Email:
Stress, depression, bi-polar disorder	Aware	aware.ie	1800 80 48 48	supportmail@aware.ie
Eating Disorders	Bodywhys	bodywhys.ie	01 2107906	alex@bodywhys.ie
Difficult times	Samaritans	samaritans.org	116 123	jo@samaritans.ie
Being a family carer	Family Carers Ireland	familycarers.ie	1800 240724	
Youth Mental Health	Jigsaw	jigsaw.ie 14 locations nationwide		
Preventing self-harm & suicide	Pieta House	pieta.ie	1800 247247	
Domestic violence and abuse by current or former partners	Women's Aid	womensaid.ie	1800 341900	helpline@womensaid.ie
Domestic violence, including coercive control	Men's Aid	mensaid.ie	01 5543811	hello@mensaid.ie

Supporting lesbian, gay, bisexual and transgender young people aged 14-23	BeLonG To	belongto.org	1890 929539	info@belongto.org
Supporting lesbian, gay, bisexual and transgender adults	LGBT Ireland	lgbt.ie	1890 929539	info@lgbt.ie
Supporting people who are affected by rape, sexual assault, harassment or childhood sexual abuse	The Rape Crisis Centre	rapecrisishelp.ie	1800 778888	
Alcohol addiction	Alcoholics Anonymous AA	alcoholicsanonymous.ie	01 8420700	gso@alcoholicsanonymous.ie
Gambling addiction	Gambler's Anonymous	gamblersanonymous.ie	01 8721133	info@gamblersanonymous.ie
Supporting older people to age at home	Alone	alone.ie	0818 222 024	hello@alone.ie

The HSE Child and Adolescent Mental Health Services (CAMHS) is a specialist service for people under the age of 18 with mental health difficulties, such as moderate to severe depression, anxiety, eating disorders and self-harm. There is further information about this service on the HSE website. www.hse.ie Your GP can make a referral for you.

The HSE National Counselling Service provides free counselling for adults who have experienced childhood abuse or neglect, medical cardholders with mild to moderate psychological difficulties and former residents of Mother and Baby Homes. Your GP can help you access this service.

If you would like to organise some private counselling sessions for yourself, the Irish Association for Counselling and Psychotherapy has a website www.iacp.ie where you can find a list of counsellors and psychotherapists in your local area.

Acknowledgements

Your soul journey. Your spiritual being. Your awakening.

Divine Energy centres around my life experience and insight. I am so grateful and privileged to have been given the opportunity to write this book which comes from eighteen years of working with clients, from babies to children and adults to the elderly. Thank you to all of my clients. I know you have been waiting patiently to get your hands on this. I'm so thankful and full of gratitude to have given you this book.

I would firstly like to show my profound gratitude to Susan Lennon Keenan for the time, dedication, support, and friendship she has given me in actively writing this book with me. Susan has been with me from the very beginning of this journey, and I would not have been able to put all of my knowledge and experience down on paper without her help, guidance, and expertise through her writing skills. Thank you so much Susan.

Thank you to the team behind me in bringing this book into your hands. Special thanks to my editor, Geraldine Walsh, for her excellent editing expertise. She gently guided me on how to structure *Divine Energy* and help it to flow more easily for you, the reader. Thank you to Orla Kelly for her publishing experience and professional input on the final publishing of this book. And thank you to my sister, Vanessa Mooney, for her excellent graphic design skills in creating the book cover for *Divine Energy*.

I would like to acknowledge two very important people who completed meditations and workshops with me through the last few years, my dear friends Mary McKiernan and Bernie McHugh who have both sadly passed away. No doubt they are in heaven laughing together saying it's about time this book is written. You are both dearly missed.

My Aunt Maura, my father's sister, was an inspiration in my life and a strong presence in this book. At a very young age, she would bring me to her house in the countryside where she would hold prayer meetings. She was a very spiritual person who had a great belief in the power of prayer. She loved to read the bible, and this helped me with my gift. I also believe in the power of prayer, the bible, and the Holy Spirt which has become a big part of my life. My Aunt Maura passed away when I was fifteen. Thank you Aunt Maura. I always feel your presence around me.

I would like to thank my partner, Charlie for all the support while writing this book. And thank you to my three sons, who I love dearly. Not forgetting, the next generation, my lovely grandchildren, I love you always, unconditionally.

On a personal note, I would like to mention my mother and father, my five brothers and seven sisters. My mother was a great inspiration and guided me through my life. She was such a considerate person dealing with all thirteen different personalities in our house with no judgement. She would sit and listen, wisely giving advice to each and everyone in the family. All of the neighbours would call to Ma Mooney as she was known. They would drop in for a cup of tea and a biscuit and she would always give them advice. This is one of the gifts I have learnt from my mother. She loves us all. She was a great singer. "Crazy" and "A Mother's Love's a Blessing" were two of the many songs she would sing. Love to both of my parents who are in heaven. Love always, your daughter Hazel.

Finally, thank you to all of my readers and clients who read this book. I'm sure you will gain powerful insight and healing as you find potential in your life through the words on these pages.

Peace, love, light, and healing.

Love Hazel

Please Review

Dear Reader,

If you enjoyed this book, would you kindly spread the word so my book can reach those who most need to hear its powerful message. If you purchased the book online, can you please post a short review on Goodreads or on whichever online store you purchased the book from? Your feedback will make all the difference to getting the word out about this book.

Thank you in advance.

Hazel